CALLED
TO
WITNESS

A Manual For
Congregational Growth

BY JERRY L. SCHMALENBERGER

C.S.S. Publishing Co., Inc.
Lima, Ohio

CALLED TO WITNESS

Copyright © 1993 by
The C.S.S. Publishing Company, Inc.
Lima, Ohio

Library of Congress Cataloging-in-Publication Data

Schmalenberger, Jerry L.
    Called to witness : a manual for congregational growth / by Jerry L. Schmalen-berger.
        108 p.   14 by 21.5 cm.
    Includes bibliographical references.
    ISBN 1-55673-558-8
    1. Church growth. 2. Evangelistic work. 3. Witness bearing (Christianity) I. Title.
BV652.25.S36   1992
254'.5—dc20   92-32743
                                                                  CIP

9306 / ISBN 1-55673-558-8   PRINTED IN U.S.A.

Dedicated to my wife, Carol, who lovingly edits, encourages and supports me in my writing and all my ministry.

Table Of Contents

Acknowledgments

The concept and content of this book have evolved over the past several years with many contributing in order for it to come to print and be made available to you.

Two administrative assistants have done the word processing and rough editing: Vernette Blumhorst, who began the whole process when I came to Pacific Lutheran Theological Seminary as its President and Professor of Parish Ministry, and Wendy Eilers, my present administrative assistant, who has not only done the bulk of the word processing, but has also contributed a great deal by doing rough editing. Without these women, the project just could not have gotten off the ground.

A portion of the book was first edited by my friend in the ELCA Division for Congregational Life, the Reverend Paul Pallmeyer. My wife, Carol Schmalenberger, who has served as the primary editor, took all of these rough-edited editions and brought them to the conclusion you see before you now. I am very thankful for the skills of all these people.

Special appreciation goes to Win Arn of the Church Growth Movement, Monrovia, California, and his good support through the entire project. Win has a passion for doing outreach in new ways during these new times. He has given me permission to quote him and his *Win Arn Growth Report* extensively so that I might apply those principles which work with our type of Christianity for making the most effective outreach program possible.

To Lyle Schaller, thanks for allowing me to quote from *Activating the Passive Church*. The editors of *Dialog* theological journal have graciously agreed to the use of my article on "Discipling." Others have agreed to be quoted as well: Jack Sims and his "Boomers Consulting;" Billie Navarro and her suggestions on parochial schools; and Paul Lintern who has a lot to say about how congregations do public relations well.

Foreword

For 29 years in my work as a parish pastor called to word and sacrament, evangelism, ministry and parish outreach have always been the highest of my priorities.

This book is an attempt to lay out many of the practical insights I have gained from hard work at outreach, including many bad ideas, false starts and disappointing results. Those things which seem to have worked well for me, I tell you about and those which did not, I give you fair warning!

During my years in parish ministry, I served the Lutheran Church in America first as a pastor evangelist and then as pastor/director of its church-wide Evangelical Outreach Emphasis. It was while preparing presentations and workshops in this capacity that I began to suspect I might have some workable solutions to offer for doing the important ministry of outreach for parish pastors who were struggling so hard to be faithful.

After receiving and accepting the call to be President and Professor of Parish Ministry of Pacific Lutheran Theological Seminary, I was able to gain a grant from Lutheran Brotherhood Foundation to establish a Center for Lutheran Church Growth and Mission on the west coast. During its first three years of experience, we have used that grant to produce material for parish pastors across the United States which we deemed would be most helpful in their ministries.

In addition, the center has carefully examined the whole church growth movement as we know it and tried to discern which of these dynamic principles of outreach resulting in growing congregations were consistent with our theology and useful to our parish pastors.

Some will also notice that I have evolved in my methodology of doing parish evangelism. My first book, published a number of years ago, titled *We Have Good News to Share*, was purely parish program oriented. This new volume I present now is a blend of three main themes: parish program emphasis church growth methodology consistent with our theology; and, most important to me as I look back on my years as an evangelist, discipling.

I now believe the number one priority for many parishes at the present time needs to emphasize moving the new member and/or new Christian from loyalty to the local organization to faithfulness in discipleship. This means responding to the call the Christ extends to us through our baptism to be ministers in the world and to be good stewards and evangelists. This work is an attempt to look at the evangelism side of that discipleship call. In the future, we'll need to examine seriously the steward's side of the same call by our Lord . . . but that's another book.

Jerry L. Schmalenberger

Critique Of The
"Church Growth Movement"

As co-chair for the Center for Lutheran Church Growth and Mission at Pacific Lutheran Theological Seminary, I am continually asked my opinion about the "church growth movement" which seems to be centered on the west coast. I believe that one of the scandals of this modern time is for many mainline denominations to simply reject all that "church growth" can teach us about reaching the unchurched and disillusioned church members amidst our present culture. Certainly it has been consistent with God's spirit that down through the years that spirit has manifested itself through many secular and less than completely spiritual institutions and centers of learning.

Perhaps a brief listing of the weaknesses and strengths, as I see them, of the church growth movement would be helpful as you select those strategies which can be effective in your particular community setting and still be consistent with your denominational and biblical theology.

One of the weaknesses of the church growth movement, as I study it, is that it seems to avoid taking any prophetic stand and tries its best to avoid all controversy. This particular tactic opposes that which the scripture implores us to be as preachers, ministers and the body of believers.

Very much misunderstood by its critics is its homogeneous principle. I, too, believe that while the homogeneous principle correctly asserts that groups grow better the more consistently alike they are, this condition does not reflect the nature of the Christian church. This principle is one we need to look at very seriously with our present cultural diversity. We must take steps to overcome that very strong resistance to becoming a part of groups which are unlike ourselves. In church growth everything is measured by numbers and statistics, something critics claim as too secular. However, the New Testament book, the Acts of the Apostles, seems to be full of numbers, many of which relate to conversions and attendance at worship experiences. In our day, these measurements are one of the tools which helps us determine effectiveness and can be used by the spirit of God as well as by the corporate, secular world.

One of my main criticisms about the church growth movement concerns a lack of appreciation for history and tradition; they would throw it all out simply to meet the needs of present-day generations. I think a more moderate line needs to be in place. On the one hand, we do need to be contemporary and take into account that which establishes contact with the needs of our unchurched friends and neighbors whom we might reach and minister to. On the other hand, we also have an obligation to convey and keep from one generation to another the rich traditions and customs which have gone on before us.

It is probably true that the church growth movement leans further toward those of our more biblically literal and fundamental sisters and brothers, a side of the spectrum farther to the right than I am comfortable with or can write about. Because of this tendency, those in the church growth movement have often the position that no way is valid but theirs, an attitude which is always suspicious in any discipline.

I also feel that many who are a part of this movement are predisposed to lean toward more simple religion, flag, country and parochialism than I would want or believe God's people should. As a world-wide family, our theology and practice of worship and evangelism ought to reflect that wholeness of God's people which is larger than any patriotism or loyalty to secular governments.

On the other hand, after saying the above, I want to put in a strong word in support of "church growth" and how it can give us new paradigms and insights into our mission and ministries.

By using church growth methodology, we can reach people where they are. The movement seems to be much more sensitive to the needs of people living in our present reality than those of us in mainline churches have been over the years. It cuts through theological jargon and worship practices which lack relevancy or are simply so far removed from present reality that they are ineffectual. Some of the denominations which are so very liturgically bound or traditionally oriented especially need this correction to make sure that all who come to worship have their needs met in a variety of ways in addition to having experienced the richness of a liturgical faith and practice.

I am especially encouraged by the priority for strong biblical emphasis and gospel/salvation language which is set and used by the church growth people. In my opinion, a number of our mainline, perhaps more liberal, denominations have all but given up basic language which states clearly such elementary ideas as salvation, redemption, forgiveness, sin and sanctification. Again, this may be a corrective that is just right for those who have leaned too far in one direction. 't is obvious to me after 29 years in the parish that those congregations which take Bible study seriously and spend program money and energy in providing the study of scripture to people with all different lifestyles are churches which will practice outreach and grow — and have their efforts rewarded.

I also believe the church growth movement provides not only excellent use of the media to proclaim the gospel with the very latest technology available to us, but also many other ways of adding life, enthusiasm and excitement to the local parish. Because with some church growth advice and techniques we can actually see growth take place, we, as clergy, are encouraged in our ministries. And since our laity can see results in their efforts to reach out, they are further motivated to do more.

Currently, the best outreach efforts for each congregation and clergy will be an eclectic gathering of strategies and actions consistent with the theology of the congregation, its creeds, confessions, and the scripture. In addition, the evangelism program should also be consistent with those elements of church growth and other sociological approaches to the community served which help us to work effectively on behalf of God's spirit, that others might know the wonderful joy we, who are God's people, know.

CHAPTER 1
Reclaiming The Witness

Reclaiming The Witness Through A Study Of The Acts Of The Apostles

That first Pentecost in the birth of the Christian church was something else! Three thousand were baptized — pity the altar guild as they tried to arrange for that service! How do you suppose the secretary got all the certificates in the right order? The ushers must have had quite a time parking all the horses, camels and chariots in the parking lot, and the property committee probably rebelled at cleaning up the mess. Think of all the baptismal candles — the acolytes had to find help carrying them. The other pastors in town probably said "the theology is weak" and "they go right on out the back door after being received into that church. Besides, we're not about church growth and numbers here."

Pentecost was something else, all right! And so was the early apostolic church.

George A. Buttrick (Walker, 109) aptly described that early church in terms of what he felt today's church is in danger of losing. First of all, they had an experience of the alive Christ which they could describe to others and a real passion to tell others about it. Their fellowship was close and meaningful — and they were changed people because of it. They could love others, even those who hated them and seemed to have an inward security and peace. And above all, there was a deep sense of joy.

I would like to take these six essentials early Christians seemed to have (according to the Book of Acts), which we may be in danger of losing in our church and look at them carefully one more time.

1. An experience of the resurrected Christ which can be described to others. Paul called this experience a mystical union and referred to it as "to be in Christ." Perhaps one of the real struggles and problems in our church today is satisfying our needs for spirituality. Our people are seeking the supernatural — they seem to have an appetite for the "other worldly." New Age religion sometimes steps in to fill the gap.

Somehow, we Christians must move beyond loyalty to an organization, the church, to be able to hear that call of discipleship, the call to be a witness. Just like Paul on the Damascus road or John on the Isle of Patmos, the alive Christ can and wants to be present with us now. The work of the Holy Spirit is more than knowing facts about Jesus. We Christians talk about sanctification, that is, becoming holy. God's promise is "and I will be with you (Matthew 28:20 TEV)."

A young lad got loose from his mother, ran down the center aisle of a performing arts auditorium during the intermission, and ran upon the stage where there was positioned a grand piano. The young lad sat down on the bench and began to play Chopsticks. When one of the stage hands running the spotlight brought it around and focused it on the young man, this new performer became very frightened. Then, slipping in through the dark stage to sit next to him on the bench was the great pianist. He began to play that other tune which blends

16

with Chopsticks above the young man's melody. He leaned over to the boy and stated: "Don't be afraid, son. I'm here with you." That is what God whispers to us as we find the spotlight of baptizing and making disciples focused on our ministries. Just as Jesus gave the commission to the disciples and promised, ". . . I will be with you to the end of the age (Matthew 28:20 TEV)," so he is with us now as we embark on this great task of telling others about the experience of the alive Christ in our own life.

For many, our present world is a place that is impersonal, cold and barren with isolation and cruelty where we often feel alone. We disciples can bring a presence of Christ which is so good for us and can be described and shared with others. In our scripture, our worship, our witness to the unchurched, our prayer and devotional life, we can become so immersed in God's presence that it just infuses and infects others around us.

In a recent ad on television for Mercedes Benz, we learn how Mercedes crashes one hundred new cars a year and then shares the results of its research on car accidents with other car makers around the world. When the engineers are asked why they would share this kind of information with their competition, the answer comes: "Some things in life are just too good not to share." You and I have something too good not to share — our experience of the resurrected Christ in our lives and the fact that we are called to witness to others about that experience.

2. A passion to tell others about it. We Christians, for the most part, have never witnessed very well. It isn't just a matter of renewing our zeal in most of the mainline churches — it is a matter of establishing, for the first time, a new paradigm which says that witnessing is one of the major ways we develop our own faith as well as that of others. Over the years we have had little passion to do this witnessing. Certainly it has not been like those disciples of Mary Kay Cosmetics or Jehovah's Witnesses.

I notice, since becoming a grandfather, that I quickly move to share that information and show those pictures when I strike up conversation with a person I've just met. If someone has recently become engaged, has a new job, or even developed a negative passion of hate or revenge for someone else, he or she moves quickly to carrying that out. It therefore seems we ought to be able to develop an even deeper, positive passion to tell others about the risen Christ.

In 1 John verses 1, 3 and 4 read: "We proclaim to you what we have seen and heard so that you also may have fellowship; and our fellowship is with God and with God's son, Jesus Christ. We write this to make our joy complete (TEV)." They experienced, so they shared. It made their joy complete in the telling. It is one of the great serendipities of being a witness to discover that the more you tell it, the more you own it and the more you own it, the better equipped you are to tell it to someone else.

In the early church they had to tell! We read these words of the account of Peter and John being arrested for teaching in a temple area: "For we cannot help speaking about what we have seen and heard (Acts 4:20 TEV)."

Let's not lose it. They seemed to have it in the early church as described in the Book of Acts of the Apostles: an experience of Christ that can be described and a passion to pass it on.

3. An unbreakable fellowship with others of the changed group. Read again, from the Book of Acts: "They devoted themselves to the Apostles' teachings and to the fellowship, to the breaking of bread, and to prayer. Everyone was filled with awe and many wonders and miraculous signs were done by the Apostles . . . and the Lord added to their numbers daily those who were being saved (Acts 2: 42, 43 and 47b TEV)." They expected great things to happen when they came together and it did. Each worship experience and gathering was a new experience loaded with possibilities. Something was going on here — and we dare not lose it — the people were moved because they were together. They knew the power of preaching, prayer, the Lord's supper. Each time they got together it was like Kellogg's Cornflakes presently says in their television ad: "Taste them again for the first time."

Early witnesses made it very clear that to become Christian meant to have changed lives — they would never be the same again. There was new power in equipping one for life itself.

In our day we must do this better or we are in danger of losing it. We dare not be another service club. To become a Christian, we need to explain to the people to whom we witness that believing means a radical change in priorities that are quite diffierent from the rest of the world's. The Dean Witter investment firm says in their ads: "We measure success one investor at a time." As we carry out our outreach efforts, we must measure our evangelism one disciple at a time as he or she receives the call to be a witness. All this means that we must make a strong emphasis of the fact that conversion and new life must be enabled as we witness to people and bring them into the body of believers.

Once when I was hunting with a very good friend, Dr. Joel Tiegland from Des Moines, Iowa, we came upon a two-strand electric fence which had to be crossed. I held his gun while he put one leg over the fence, believing it was not electrified. As soon as he stood straddling the fence, he discovered it was hot! The shock was strong enough that he could not get his other leg over the fence or return to the original side of the fence. So, there my friend Joel jumped. He went from one foot to the other while the fence continued to shock him.

The very next week I had a meaningful time talking in my pulpit about the fact that we live in two worlds as God's people. But more significant to my peers that day was the fact that we talked about how painful it is to be part of the body of Christ, which is the church, and to attempt to continue living in both the world and in the church. Discipleship calls for an unbreakable fellowship with the others of the changed group. We need to look carefully at all the change which needs to happen.

So we must have a close, meaningful fellowship of changed people, a passion to tell others, and an experience of the alive Christ which we can describe to others.

4. A love of people not dependent on being loved or even liked, an unbreakable good will. The radical element of the early church which kept the adrenalin pumping, this principle kept the people coming back and bringing others. It was the vision, the mission, the challenge which brought and kept excitement alive and vital. It gave a sense of direction and great purpose to the cause.

We must reclaim the apostolic radical dimension of our faith. Jew, gentile, slave, free, male, female, black, white, soldier and captive were all included. Just look at that list, provided for us in Acts, of different nationalities baptized on Pentecost. The early church of the apostles and disciples was a rich mix of all sorts and kinds of people. People of color and of differing languages, nationalities, and tribes were all included. See in that same church James, Lydia, Simon of Cyrene, Alexander and Rufus, Mary Magdalene, Martha, Peter, James, the Ethiopian eunuch, Cornelius and so forth. Inclusivity isn't some new fad to be tried. It was at the heart of the radical New Testament apostolic church.

And what a group we have to love on God's behalf today in order to be consistent with the apostolic church: the abused, the homeless, Iraqi and Israeli, Arab and Jew, Muslim and Christian, those who demonstrate against war, and those who demonstrate to celebrate. We must include the criminal in a culture which wants every deviant locked up and the powerless or drug-addicted whom some would do away with. Those who have made a mess of their lives, their spouses, and kids, and who don't deserve a thing from us, we love anyway.

During the Persian Gulf War, Peter Jennings on ABC News told the story of an Iraqi family living in Indiana who had named their first son Saddam Hussein. During the Persian Gulf War a second son was born and they named him George Bush. When asked by Jennings why they would name the second son George Bush, the comment was made that they hoped Hussein and Bush could be brothers.

A love of people not dependent on being loved or even liked, an unbreakable good will is that which the early church had and what we, as God's people, must continue to maintain. So we reclaim that all encompassing radical love which includes those who don't deserve to be loved; we continue a fellowship unbreakable with the others of the changed group; and we develop a passion to describe to others our experience of the alive Christ.

5. *An inward security or peace not dependent on the number of things we get done in a day.* I really have a long way to go in order to claim for myself this principle of the early church! I am such a driven person that when I accomplish something during the day I hadn't planned to do, I go back to my desk and add that task to my "to do" list for the day and mark it out, so I can feel good about all I've achieved when the day is over! Yet, this Shalom of God is one of the great gifts we have to offer. We all have a story to tell of the peace that we can come to our own life with God's presence.

Today we live in a pressure-cooker society full of frustration, competition, war, crime, drugs, hate, peer-pressure, quotas, fear and distrust, job loss, depression, fragmentation and complicated cultural situations. In a situation like this, we have God's peace to give.

My wife, Carol, tells a humorous story about hurrying to get our children ready for Sunday school one morning after I had already left to conduct the two earlier worship services. She hurried the kids into the station wagon in the garage, raised the door and backed out. As she drove into town (probably faster than she should have) they heard a scratching sound on the roof of the station wagon, like fingernails on a blackboard. Before long, the noise had moved to the back of the roof and suddenly a cat's tail appeared in the rear window. That cat had tried its best to hang on against the wind's pressure after being caught napping on top of the station wagon and surprised at her sudden swift ride!

Often we, and certainly many of the people to whom we witness, are hanging on like that cat. In such a setting, we have a mission of peace around us to those struggling with their marriage, out of money, afraid of a terminal illness, addicted to wealth or power, single parenting, wealthy and unfilled, drug addicted, sexually uncontrolled, alone or full of guilt.

We have a gospel of peace to all those cats going downhill and barely hanging on. We have a mission of peace to those warring wherever they may be: in our homes, churches, neighborhoods, country or around the world.

In the movie *Out of Africa,* Denys says that map makers, when they got to the edge where they knew nothing, would write: "Beyond this place there be demons and dragons." Many of our people live in that world of demons and dragons and we can bring security and peace.

Like Jesus calmed the storm of Galilee, we also can bring calm to those who are in storms in their own lives. It's an inward security and peace we have, a radical love of others, an unbreakable fellowship of changed people, a passion to tell other people about the experience of the living Christ in our own lives.

6. *A deep sense of joy not dependent on being happy, for joy is not the opposite of unhappiness, but the opposite of unbelief.* Joy is what we are chosen for and joy is what we offer to all who will come. And that joy is not just the absence of trouble, but rather the presence of God in our lives. In Philippians 4 we read "Rejoice in the Lord always. I will say it again: Rejoice — do not be anxious about anything, but in everything, by prayer and petition, with thanksgiving, present your request to God. And the peace of God, which transcends all understanding, will guard your hearts and your minds in Christ Jesus (Philippians 4:4, 6, 7 TEV)."

We Christians must be careful, for in our attempt to be sincere, we may give a totally different picture. It can appear as if Christianity means long faces, closed minds, sad stories, difficult hymns, and almost morbid worship, Jesus likened being a disciple to being part of a wedding reception, not a funeral procession!

In an interview with Amy Grant on CNN when asked about the purpose of Christian music, she responded simply, "It is to lift people up."

Only two percent of recordings sold in 1990 was of classical music. No wonder Charles Wesley and Martin Luther used tunes from the taverns and common music of their day!

There is a playful, fun, delighted-to-be-here kind of nature to the Christian faith — and God's presence as well. This ought to be obvious in our worship and our entire ministry. Jesus said in John 15: "I have told you this so that my joy may be in you and that your joy may be complete (v. 11 TEV)."

Let's recapture that joy today. See if you can find joy in the telling of the story and in being together for this experience.

We should have joy because the creator of the whole universe cares about us. We are part of God's saved family through our baptism. Ultimately we are saved right on into eternity. We know forgiveness and thus relief from haunting guilt and we have God's presence to see us through in the present and the meantime.

That's how it is to be a Christian. It's the way it was back in the days of the Book of Acts of the Apostles, and the way we can be right now in this world.

George A. Buttrick described it as something the early church had and something he feared we were in danger of losing in our church today:

•a deep sense of joy not dependent on being happy

•an inward security or peace not dependent on the number of things we get done in a day

•a love of people not dependent on being loved or even liked

•an unbreakable fellowship with the others of the changed group

•a passion to tell others about it

•an experience of the alive Christ that we can describe to others.

Reclaiming The Witness Through Discipling

What person called to witness wouldn't like to better integrate new Christians into the congregation, practice good

23

membership conservation (so that members remain faithful in the body of Christ) and produce more people and money for mission and ministry?

Who in the congregation wouldn't like to see the spiritual life of individual members deepened, to develop a large group of lay volunteers for parish ministry, to identify which un-churched people are most open to becoming members, and give the individual member a sense of doing what he or she has been called by God to do in the first place?

The above scene can take place in congregations if we are willing to explore the significance of Jesus' command to the disciples on the Mount of Ascension where he told them to "Go . . . make them my disciples . . . (Matthew 28:19 TEV)." It's called discipling, and it deals with that aspect of our minis-try which takes place with our new members as they join the congregation and immediately thereafter. We pastors need to examine the manner in which we equip these folks to be mem-bers of the church.

It seems that the length of the Inquirer's Class (or Pastor's Class, as some call it) has become noticeably shorter. In many parishes it has dwindled to no more than a brief reception at the time the person joins the congregation to teach the new members about "the way we do things here at St. John's." This approach only builds loyalty to the organization.

This method of integrating new members into the congre-gation may have been adequate several years ago when denominational congregations were simply receiving "their own" from other locations. However, now that we live and evangelize in a pluralistic society where already converted denominational Christians do not seek out their "own peo-ple," a change is called for.

What is needed is a fresh approach to discipling new (or renewed) Christians when they become part of that family of God called the congregation. We must discover how best to move these new members beyond simple loyalty to a congre-gation into a loyalty to Christ and a faithfulness to the call of their baptism to be ministers in the world as well.

24

You know how it often goes. The inquirer attends four to six classes on Sunday morning or some other time during the week and is duly received into the congregation by baptism, confirmation, letter of transfer or affirmation of faith. On the same Sunday the new member is received, an usher hands him or her a box of offering envelopes and a time and talent card which serve as recruitment tools to encourage service in the nursery, on the youth committee or the church council, as an usher or a youth activities sponsor. No doubt the women's organization will approach the females and invite them to a group meeting.

If we are going to be serious about being a faithful Christian, true to the call of making disciples, a lot more is called for than this rather perfunctory claim on a person's life to be loyal to a local congregation.

The following diagram is an attempt to show our reasons for doing evangelism and stewardship, indicate appropriate responses to what God has done for us, list some ways Christians live out their faith, and provide some "levels" where members tend to be in spiritual maturity.

GOD'S ACTION

Blesses   Saves

Baptism

The Church

Commitment

STEWARDSHIP   EVANGELISM

Lifestyle

Discipleship

Shares   Witnesses

OUR RESPONSE

The diagram on page 25 puts God's action at the top, which is certainly a claim toward the divine initiative to which we Christians adhere. The bottom section is our response to what God has done for us. In between, I have named some groups of Christians I have observed in my 29 years in the parish, and, for the last several years, as Professor of Parish Ministry at Pacific Lutheran Theological Seminary.

The Baptized

Many members of our congregations are simply loyal to their denomination because of the nationality or ethnic groupings of their ancestors. They attend church rarely, but know to which congregation they belong and can name their denomination at once if a census taker asks them at the door. They were baptized, just as their children will be, because that's what their families have always done and they want to be faithful to that tradition. They know that by being baptized, they are members of the congregation, and as such, will not hesitate to requisition the congregation's help at times of disaster and crisis in their lives.

The Committed

Another group I have observed in my ministry might be called "The Committed." Not unlike people who are committed to a service organization like Kiwanis or Rotary or to a baseball team like the Cincinnati Reds or the Oakland Athletics, these folks are piously committed to a local congregation and perhaps even a denomination of Christians as a whole. They will sign the pledge card and provide the income necessary to keep good old First Church open, no matter what! They will practice a tiny bit of witness in their lives in order to maintain a crowd big enough to keep the church doors open. They and their families attend church regularly. They are the lifeblood of our congregations at present.

Lifestyle

While the Committed may or may not have a certain spiritual depth, there is yet another group of people whose spirituality runs deep. Their lifestyles are profoundly implicated by their beliefs which are reflected every day of the week in how they live out their existence in the world. It's a tremendous joy to help a new member move beyond simply being committed to the cause of the church to that of integrating their beliefs into his or her daily life. While their numbers are small in most of our congregations, often they are the source of deep satisfaction (and sometimes abrasive irritation) to congregations and pastors alike. These folks want to see that "their walk is equal to their talk" and often call for the same kind of consistency in congregational ministry and mission as they are trying to live out in their own lives: integrating the call of their baptism and their daily life activities. They want their pastor to be more than a "professional," a "manager," or an "enabler" — they want a spiritual guide.

Discipleship

There may be a few members who are responding to their call to discipleship. This is a new area of ministry for many Christians, but one which can change dramatically our ability to witness and practice stewardship in the world. Discipling means that the pastor will intentionally help new members who have entered into the fellowship of the congregation to respond faithfully to their call through their baptism to be ministers in the world all week long and to be witnesses and stewards in all that they do. The pastor is their spiritual director.

Discipling means spending as much congregational money and energy with new members after they join the congregation as is spent in wooing them there in the first place. Discipling means that it might be best to receive our new member students into the congregation halfway through the inquirer's

27

class series and spend the second half of the series developing themes of lay ministry, evangelism and stewardship. People who join the church would then learn how to witness to their faith, would become motivated to tithe their income, and would know well the implications of managing all the natural resources God has provided to us as God's people here on this earth. Stewardship of health, life, gifts, and time would be well thought out as they continue to mature in their spirituality.

Church growth people, like Win Arn of Pasadena, California, have taught us that new members are by far the best witnesses to reach others. They invariably know six to eight unchurched people, who may be acquaintances, relatives or co-workers. New members, if instructed well in witnessing, are the best potential evangelists in our congregation, and thus are the best source of names and addresses of unchurched people who would be most likely to join if approached and invited. The pastor who works with them in their continued spiritual growth will see big dividends for them, the congregation, the kingdom and the pastor.

In my former parish, St. John's Lutheran Church in Des Moines, Iowa, I was thrilled to learn that new members, upon being received into the congregation, were quite willing to stick with the instruction class for additional time in order to learn how to witness to their faith. They knew more unchurched people than long-time members seemed to know and would then go out into the community to share the good news with their friends and family. In addition, these new members were more open to considering what the call to be a steward and witness in the scripture really means.

For the first six months after a person joined my congregation in Des Moines, they were expected to serve on the "Calling Squad," which met with me on Sunday afternoons (see chapter 3 — "Congregational Witness Through a Calling Squad"). The Calling Squad learned how to witness to its faith (which involved practicing out loud at the church), took part in Bible study, and then called on prospective members in their homes. That same Sunday evening they would meet with me for fellowship at a local restaurant, where, through sharing our experiences, we became even closer to each other. That period of witnessing for six months after they joined took advantage of their enthusiasm and excitement about their faith, and the fact that new members are best acquainted with the "extended congregation" (that group of people who have not yet joined, but are related in some way to present members).

On one occasion, new member adults on the calling squad generated so much excitement that their children asked if they could have their own youth calling squad. And they did!

If we take seriously this point of entry into the membership of our congregations and try to do discipling, it not only means teaching our new members how to practice stewardship of their money, time and bodies, but also practicing "gift identification" (something our more fundamentalist brothers and sisters have practiced for a long time). Consulting with members of their family — and certainly their peers — we must help new Christians discover how God has gifted them with special abilities and skills. The pastor then helps them discover ways to use those gifts and skills out in the world all week long where they work, live and play. Discipling is a much deeper approach than the traditional one of handing out "time, talent and treasure" cards to be filled out by new members the first day they join.

Developing Spirituality

Discipling also means learning how to be spiritual guides for other people. A firm in Placentia, California, which has researched the babyboomer generation, asked that group what they looked for in a congregation before they would consider joining it (see *Through Reaching Secular People*). Their top preference was a congregation which could "get them in touch with the supernatural." Well — that's our business! That is what we ought to do best! Getting in touch with the supernatural is what we clergy are called to do for others and for ourselves. We need to take much more seriously the opportunities to meet frequently with our new members to equip them to deepen their spiritual lives through study of the word, frequent worship and daily meditation and prayer. Getting in touch with the supernatural ought to be our strong suit, anyway! I am confident that if the word gets out in a community that a particular congregation and pastor are able to change individuals' lives by deepening them spiritually, the congregation will grow by leaps and bounds!

When new members learn that the "Are you saved, brother?" style of witnessing isn't necessarily the only approach, perhaps they will be much more willing to risk a witness lifestyle out in the world. If we can help them express their faith in a non-threatening way through interpersonal witnessing, we can remove much of the anxiety and fear that many have had in doing evangelism over the years.

Through discipling and teaching our people to move on through simply baptized membership, on beyond the commitment to the cause or institution, and even further to that of the integration of a lifestyle consistent with what we believe, we can respond to God's call to be a disciple and witness in this world.

This also means moving our folks beyond the idea that all they need to do is give their money to the church in order to support a cause to which they are loyal. We can help them begin to see a much more wholesome concept of stewardship: one which says that "my need to give my money away is more important than any church's need to have it." The new (or renewed) member's response to God's action will be much more satisfying and consistent with the scripture than to pleas for loyalty to the institution.

Perhaps we pastors might even look at this diamond (see diagram on page 25) to determine where we are, and consider moving to a level, then our ministry will not only integrate new members into the congregation, but will also practice good membership conservation. Our members will remain in the body of Christ, witnessing and practicing stewardship.

Is it possible to deepen the spiritual life of our congregation, develop a large group of lay volunteers for ministry in the parish, identify those unchurched people who are most open to becoming members, and provide many new members and much more money for mission and ministry? Discipling could be the answer. At least if it were practiced by us baptized, we could be assured we were doing what God has called us to do. According to Matthew's account of the great commission, Jesus told those first disciples, ''Therefore go and make disciples of all nations, baptizing them in the name of the Father, and of the Son, and of the Holy Spirit (Matthew 28:19 NIV).'' If that seems like a tall order, remember he also promised: ''and surely I am with you always . . . (Matthew 28:20).'' In being faithful to our calling to follow Christ as a disciple, others just might follow our example!

In the remainder of this book I will address our responses as pictured on one side of the diamond. That response will be the witness of the disciple. Stewardship will be left to volume two.

31

CHAPTER 2
Congregational Witness

Congregational Witness Through Goal Setting

The nature of ordained ministry is such that we can always find plenty to do to fill every moment of every day of every week of the year. If we're going to be faithful to our calling — to fully proclaim God's gospel and be evangelists — then it becomes crucial that we set our own personal goals and enable the congregational members to set theirs as well.

Please remember that congregational goals are only as worthwhile as the congregation as a whole believes in the ownership of those goals. A process must be developed for as many members of the congregation as possible to take part in establishing the annual goals for accomplishing evangelism. Small study groups, women's organizational groups, functional committees of the congregation, the church council, and the church staff (in larger congregations), all ought to have a part in establishing attainable and measurable goals for the membership.

After working this process through its broadest possibilities, the goals can be voted on by the entire congregation at the annual meeting of the congregation. In 1976 the Evangelical Outreach Emphasis of the Lutheran Church in America and the American Lutheran Church established the following five goals which make excellent congregational goals. Remember, though, these cannot be handed down by the pastor or evangelism committee or church council. They must come up through the ranks of the membership and be recommended to the congregation for vote through the congregational council. Stated simply, these were the goals:

1. *Affirm the commitment of members to be witnesses to the gospel.* Surprising as it may seem, many Christians still have to be convinced that it's a good thing to witness to Christ in the world. Probably because of the obnoxious ways of some of our fundamentalist brothers and sisters, many other Christians simply will not take part in such activity. From the preaching and teaching in the parish, and also from the evangelism committee, there needs to be a strong affirmation that this is a good, right and expected thing those called to be witnesses will do.

2. *Seek out all the unchurched.* Notice that the emphasis can be on all. For many, it is common practice to think of our people as opposed to the rest of civilization. In a day of multicultural experience and globalization, we simply must consider all people of all ethnic backgrounds, languages and colors who are unchurched to be the object of our effective proclamation and witness.

3. *Seeking to recover inactive members.* A large portion of people in any of our communities will be folks who have had bad experiences in our or other congregations and now consider themselves inactive. We must be very cautious that we do not spend all of our people resources and energy going after this kind of person. It is the most difficult ministry of all! We must do it because it is pastoral, and Christ would have us do it. However, we need to send the highly skilled and trained who are very loyal to the pastor and congregation to

34

do this kind of work. We can easily burn out members who are enthusiastic, but not well equipped, to carry out this vital but difficult ministry.

Nearly half a congregation's new members begin to become inactive after the first 18 months of membership. This means that there are large numbers of inactive people everyone knows around and in neighborhoods where we live.

Dr. John Savage's little book titled *The Bored and Apathetic Church Member,* will give us good techniques for positive ways of trying to recover and understand this large group of Christians who are uncommitted to any congregation.

4. Integrating new and restored members into the Christian community. Finding the best way to integrate new members into the fellowship after helping them to join the membership is one of the most vital ministries for which we need to strategize in a local congregation. This process accomplished well cuts down on the number of those who go inactive from any congregation. Because nationally many Christians become inactive shortly after they join congregations, it is an important goal for which we need to set a specific intentional strategy.

5. Enlist and equip members for verbal witness. Perhaps here is where we most often fall down in our congregational planning. Certainly every group of God's believers should offer, at least once a year, an opportunity for their members to equip themselves to give witness to the Christian faith out in the world where they live, play and are employed. I'll have more about this later.

Setting goals such as these gives an intentionality to our evangelism efforts in the congregation and provides us something to measure against at each witness task force meeting and parish council gathering. It is not good enough simply to list the five goals without putting numbers to them to measure against. We must see when we've reached the goal and be able to measure our progress in the meantime. For example, this would mean that with Goal 1 we might place an objective like preaching five sermons on the subject of witnessing

35

in which we affirm the commitment of our members to do just that.

Under Goal 2 we could decide to bring 50 new adult members and their children into the congregation by year's end.

For Goal 3 have a realistic expectation of recovering perhaps eight inactive members, not only bringing them back to the church as active participants, but seeing that they are fully integrated into the fellowship and are discipled.

Goal 4 can be further carried out by setting the objective of seeing that all new members received are assigned individual sponsors from the congregation. Conducting a six-month check-up by telephone for each new member that year, as well as having a one-year's celebration of belonging to the congregation is an additional objective.

Goal 5 might suggest that a congregation equip and commission one of its members to teach witnessing and then set out to teach and model it in half of the organized groups of the congregation over a period of one year, as well as doing this same thing for each confirmation and new member class received into formal membership.

If you are a pastor, you also need to set personal goals. As one called to witness, you'll want to take your obligation seriously. This means covenanting with the parish council and pastoral relations committee that a specified number of hours each week will be allocated in your ministry to doing evangelism work. A reasonable expectation might be eight hours per week. This is measurable, attainable, and it calls to attention, in the pastor's reporting to the council, just how high a priority this work has in that particular congregation.

In setting such personal goals by baptizing at least 10 new adult Christians in a year, we have something we can strive toward and can measure our success along the way. Because baptizing an adult cannot be "stealing sheep" from another congregation or simply moving Christians from one congregation to another, counting adult baptisms can be a measurable way of accounting for witness activity for most pastors.

While some may argue that these are very mechanical ways of measuring evangelism and reduces it to simply getting new members for the congregation, one might also claim that goals keep the witness priority high in our own personal ministries and in the program of the parish.

Congregational Witness Through Organization

To get started as called witnesses, discover what new members perceive the congregation's strengths to be and what attractiveness it already has going for it. One of the first things that can be done is to conduct a survey of the people who have joined the congregation in the last two years.

We need to find God's affirmation in the congregation's strengths for attracting and serving new people and capitalize on those strengths. Then in a second survey study the neighborhood to determine how those in it might be reached in an effective manner (see Chapter 3). This method gives us some little victories and progress that will be important to celebrate as new members come to the congregation.

Enlist a group of members who will pray for all the efforts in outreach. Let's not underestimate the power of the Holy spirit working through members of the congregation who may be unable to help in any other way.

Begin at once to preach the good news from the pulpit (see Chapter 5), affirming that we are called to be evangelists and witnesses. Give specific examples of people who have come into the Christian faith and how it affects their lives. Tell your own experience of the Christian faith and how equipping and freeing it is for you and your family. Keep that good news good, inspirational and interesting from the pulpit.

Recruit a special task force for a specific length of time, each person having his or her own task, for addressing the needs of witness in your neighborhood and community. Don't leave this up to those who volunteer. It is better to go after the top-notch people in the congregation who have lots of skills, talents and abilities and who are already busy people because of them. Be sure these talented members know what their job is and when they have accomplished it. It is imperative that they know when they will be finished with their responsibilities on that committee.

Sample Organization For Congregational Witness

Larger Congregations	Smaller Congregations
Parish Council	Parish Council
Witness Task Force:	Evangelism Task Force:
Chair (council person)	Chair
New member integration	Pastor & calling squad
Secretary	Secretary & telephone
Evangelism education	Inactive & new member
Telephone	integration
Inactive inreach	New member classes
New member classes	and witness
Youth witness	education
Calling squad	Youth witness
Pastor	

As many different groups in the parish as possible should be educated in the need for and ways to witness. A member of the evangelism task force can have the responsibility of visiting as many organized groups as possible, motivating and instructing them on evangelism possibilities that God has called them to do in this particular fellowship.

Develop a "responsibility" list. This means opening up as many channels as possible to get names and addresses of persons for whom the committee members will take the responsibility to share the Christian faith and/or will invite to be a part of your congregational fellowship. In small communities these names can come from Welcome Wagon, utility company hookups of people newly moved into the community, "neighborhood spies" who are members of your congregation and will phone in the names and addresses of new people, and references from the referral service of your denomination. While newcomers to the community are an important source of names, remember those five to seven unchurched people who live in your service area and who are well-known by your present congregational members. (When listed together, these five to seven unchurched people for each member you have make up the extended congregation.) That responsibility list is crucial and must be kept up-to-date, and augmented regularly. All these people should receive the regular parish newsletter and appropriate mailings of the congregation and be visited often.

It is important to identify visitors at the worship services and do a follow-up the same week that they attend. Ours is often a lifestyle where everyone in the home works and lives in an apartment building that's impossible to enter unannounced. In such situations the first approach can be done by telephone within a day or so after they attend the worship service as a visitor. Their response can give an indication of the propriety of making a home visit by the evangelism task force rather than the pastor. We don't want to embarrass the visitors at the worship service, but we do want to make certain to take notice of them and provide a proper welcome.

Schedule a class about baptism and be ready to teach it. In addition, set up a series of classes, (each with a different format) for people who would like to inquire further about the Christian faith. It is important that you spend as much time in this class with the students after they join the congregation as before. The first half of the series of classes should cover the basics of the Christian faith. This second part of the class series should stress training them to be witnesses, stewards and faithful church members.

Outline For Inquirer's Class

   1. Getting to know Each Other and an Introduction to the Church
   2. The Sacraments and Rites of the Church
   3. The Scriptures: Old and New Testament

4. The Reformation and Confessions (or Church History and Statements of Belief)

5. The Creeds and Ways to Join and Receive Members into the Church

6. Discipleship: Stewardship and Evangelism

7. Christian Worship: Listening to the Sermon

8. Basic Beliefs: Nice Things to Know About God

9. Right or Wrong for Christians

10. Witnessing to Others and Getting Organized to Do It

Be a good steward to members who move from your congregation to another community and notify the pastor and congregation in that community and the referral service of your denomination. Follow up faithfully on those people who leave with just as much enthusiasm as you do for those people who might join your congregation.

After a period of time, if your members who have moved have not transferred to another congregation, write to them or give them a phone call, encouraging them to transfer.

Congregational Witness Through Worship

The worship experience each week is not only for the congregation's members who have gathered to be encouraged and hear again the good news they already know so well. It is also for those who are not members of Christ's body or familiar with the congregation's traditional worship patterns. Since the worship must be geared to both, there will always be some tensions in worship planning, such as these on a continuum:

Equipping the saints	Saving the unsaved
The familiar routine	Contemporary variety
Communion (sacramental)	Proclamation (homiletical-preaching)
Denominational	Ecumenical
Sermon instruction	Sermon invitation and announcement
Easy hymns	Meaningful hymn words
Appreciation of ancient	Free and contemporary

40

Thinking (intellectual)	Feeling (emotional)
Bible centered	Contemporary narrative
Led by the pastor (professional)	Lay participation (volunteer)
Slavery to rubrics	Lone ranger
Solemnity and contemplation	Joy and serendipity
Conversational	Inspirational
Affirmation of the old	Attraction of the new
Soul saving for the future	Justice and mercy now
Purists, traditionalists in music	Freedom, frivolity and poor theology in music

A representative worship committee and pastor who can hold the above tensions in perspective and make certain that all the people of God have their needs met will be very valuable to any parish's spiritual health and outreach efforts.

The hour we schedule worship is also crucial. Certainly it is not wise to change already established and successful worship services. However, because lifestyles have changed so drastically in recent years, we ought to consider Saturday night, Wednesday noon, or Thursday evening services as well where the format can be less formal. Many parishes are finding that an early Saturday evening service is well attended by a variety of members and visitors, as well as older people in the community. It is an excellent time to marry those who request a rather private service. Some congregations also do much of their baptizing at this Saturday evening service.

Signs throughout the building and the parking lot ought to be welcoming signs and should not threaten those people who are attending.

Ushers and greeters need to be well trained, not to look like wooden soldiers, but to be genuinely friendly and helpful especially to the person attending for the first or second time. They should represent various ages, male and female, single and married.

A number of practices at worship can help witness take place. First of all, make the experience celebrative in nature. This is especially true at times of adult baptisms and reception of new members.

For those attending who do not know our Christian "shop talk," the worship bulletin or program needs to be easily read and followed. Keep this in mind in your choice of words.

It's important that the music selected is both easy to sing and carries the tradition of our worship for which so many people long. We simply have to remember that the laity rarely consider the theology or significance of the words in contrast to their delight in singing the melody of our hymns.

Since our preaching ought not assume that anyone present was there last week, the sermon should be a self-contained unit to enable the person attending for the first time to make sense out of it and feel invited by God into the kingdom fellowship (see Chapter 5).

Put in place a sure-fire method of recognizing all our visitors and getting their names and addresses. Having the visitor at worship stand and introduce himself or herself may not be the wisest thing to do. Often first-time visitors, if they have come to the service because of crisis in their lives, are not comfortable and may be embarrassed giving their names and other information publicly. If a person has been brave enough to approach our church worship service to attend, then he or she is certainly an ideal prospect for catechizing and bringing into the Christian faith.

Be sure to seek the counsel of the unchurched in the area when making decisions about worship practice. When we ask only those people who are already in attendance, we have narrowed considerably the group of people to whom we will be relevant and serve through worship.

Frequent surveys of the congregation, including the extended congregation (see Chapter 5), those not presently attending, and the unchurched in the community, will help in planning worship which meets their needs adequately.

Baptism And Outreach

Because we Christians view baptisms as the initiatory rite into the community of the saved and a celebration of how

God forgives and adopts into God's family, let's give very special attention to how we conduct the baptismal sacrament and how we prepare for it.

Perhaps one of the most fertile opportunities for witnessing to our faith and instructing people in the good news is in preparing sponsors, parents and godparents to take part in the baptismal service. This ought to be done in an unhurried fashion as we instruct these folks in the significance of both the Old Testament and New Testament covenants and God's initiative in our being part of the saved.

While not true in every ministry setting, some pastors believe they can judge how well their ministry is going by the number of adult baptisms they do in any given year. This statistic reflects the area in which we are placing our energy, as it literally counts the new Christians for whom we have been a part in bringing into the kingdom.

If we can accept this idea, then reporting baptisms (especially adult baptisms) ought to have first line, top priority in parish council and in annual meeting reports. It should be mentioned frequently in the prayer of the church at the altar. We ought to place the baptismal font in an obvious, strategic location so that the congregational members are reminded of how important this sacrament really is.

The service of affirmation of baptism is called for several times during the church year and can be a very meaningful experience. Make it an instrument through which the spirit of God motivates people to share the good news of this sacrament with those who have not yet had opportunity to receive it.

Make sure that every person in your congregation knows his or her baptismal date and uses that date as much as possible. Greet your people with a greeting card or phone call on the anniversary of their baptism. At the sacrament of infant baptism, present a candle which can be used to celebrate this child's baptismal day annually at home. On the liturgical day of the Baptism of our Lord which comes right after Epiphany, everyone can celebrate his or her own baptism.

When we use the Apostles' Creed in the worship setting, we can introduce that creed by saying it is a statement of what all the baptized here hold in common.

And most of all: Find the unbaptized! Begin with your own family and search for relatives; include friends, folks in the local jail, counselees, participants in weddings and funerals, worship visitors, your children's friends at school and social acquaintances. Don't forget that extended congregation: those friends, family and co-workers of your present membership.

People will respond to an advertisement in a local newspaper inviting them to inquire about what's necessary to be baptized into the Christian faith in your congregation. An unthreatening telephone number they can call to make further inquiries will get repeated use.

Holding special public baptisms, such as in a lake at a public beach on a holiday like the 4th of July, will be a visual aid showing that we Christians take this sacrament very seriously. You can instruct your candidates for baptism and get them ready to make this very first witness in their life by being a part of a very public demonstration of its worthiness.

Congregational Witness Through Developing Prospects

The very best prospects for new members of your congregation will be found in the families and friendships of your present newer members. Query the newer members to discover the potential seven or eight prospective members they know and put those names and addresses on your responsibility list. There will always be a number of unchurched people within these webs or networks of those who have already joined the church. However, the longer a member is with a congregation, the fewer unchurched friends he or she is likely to have as potential members.

The above principle is the reason it's so important to program the congregtion for those people who are potential members of the congregation as well as those who have already joined. This makes identifying those people within the webs of newer members crucial.

One pastor, whose congregation has grown rapidly, tells about how she always visits the unchurched friends of her new members within the first few weeks after they have joined the church! Another congregation regularly places slips of paper in the worship bulletin asking its members to list several people they know who are unchurched, and if they will call on them or whether other members of the congregation should make the witnessing visit.

Congregational Witness Through Enabling Members

Witness Instruction Opportunities

There are a number of times during the parish program year when organized groups are already available for witness instruction. The person on the Outreach Task Force who has accepted the responsibilty of witness education can take advantage of these already organized groups and ask to be invited to one of their sessions when witness instruction can be offered.

The following groups will be receptive to a brief period of instruction:

church council
youth groups
Bible study groups
new members' classes
women's and men's organized groups
choirs
confirmation classes
church school classes (adult and youth)

Retreat As An Opportunity To Grow

For those members of the congregation called to be witnesses, a day or two away from the parish can be valuable in motivating them to learn how to be witnesses where they work, play and live. Retreats away from the church building give intentional time for reflection, renewal and spiritual deepening which just do not happen in the busy schedule of our daily lives or even the program schedule of our parishes. Here is a suggested schedule for such a retreat:

The first evening:
opening worship
getting to know each other
study session 1
evening prayer

The next morning:
breakfast
prayer time
study session 2
break time
study session 3

In the afternoon:
lunch
time to relax
study session 4
organized recreation
dinner
prayer time
study session 5
first steps to take back home
prayer and dismissal

While you will probably get the best results and the most interest in attending the retreat by recruiting a task force to set up the program content, here is one possible idea which may be helpful in a discipling approach. The theme idea came from *Toward Developing An Evangelistic Lifestyle* (American Baptist Churches in the USA). The following aims are not "steps" and do not need to be done in any special order. They are signs that we are living out our baptism in the "good news" lifestyle. The title of the retreat might be "The Good News Way of Life." The study sessions would take up the following marks of an evangelistic lifestyle:

1. Repentance. We see the difference between the way we are and the way we ought to be and learn to express sorrow for the way our lives thwart God's will being done. We then turn our lives around. Bible study of Jonah 1 and Luke 19:1-10.

2. Affirmation. We recognize that despite our personal and corporate sin, God's "yes" is stronger than our "no." We learn to affirm each other. Bible study of Jonah 2, Isaiah 9:2-9 and Matthew 28:16-20.

46

3. Proclamation. The good news lifestyle includes telling the truths of God for all to hear in every setting. Study 1 John 1:1-2 and 10.

4. Invitation. This involves calling forth decisions, gifts and responses of others, so they, too, will become what God intends for them. Study Isaiah 55 and Matthew 11:28-30.

5. Celebration. We learn of the sense of joy and gladness, playfulness and mystery, in the good news lifestyle. Study Psalms 146 and 150.

6. Commitment. We consider a shift in allegiance from our patterns of living to those showing commitment to God's pattern of discipleship. We'll also consider our stewardship. Study Matthew 10:34-42.

A sermon series by this author on the above themes (especially appropriate during Lent) and an accompanying Bible study to go with each one may be obtained from C.S.S. Publishing, Lima, Ohio, and is titled *The Good News Way of Life.*

A retreat is often much more valuable if the participants are gathered together after three to four weeks following to have a debriefing on their success in carrying out that which they learned and vowed to do upon returning home. This can be a celebrative evening meal in someone's home or at the church, for encouragement to those who are trying to live out a life of evangelism and witness. In many instances, groups will develop into a regular fellowship which will meet monthly and give each other support.

Witness Through Renewal Of The Passive Congregation

Some observers of our congregations claim that up to 80 percent of them may be in a state of passivity. Poorly organized to do outreach, passive congregations are almost always weak in their efforts. Usually they are ineffective in discipling, as the vertical relationship between God and individual is most often neglected. When congregations lose sight of mission strategy and mission for the future, this passivity takes hold where most of their energy and talents is spent remembering the good old days. The enthusiasm which may have once been there to do outreach by inviting others into the fellowship of the congregation wanes, and the congregation declines in membership and worship attendance. This often leads to a blase attitude about congregational activities and low self esteem as a family of God.

Renewal for the passive congregation has to begin with spiritual renewal. This can be accomplished by daily or weekly study of the scripture, retreats which produce disciples out of those members who have only been loyal to the congregation in the past and never quite matured in their faith.

As you design your congregation's move out of passivity, it will take some very intentional strategy and planning from strength. Avoid the trap of getting all the programs going that have been neglected and diminished over the years from when the congregation was in its prime. Instead, we should begin by affirming those programs which already have some strength and build upon those.

Little celebrations of accomplishments will do great things for congregational life and vigor. Set attainable goals. When they are reached, be sure to tout them to the congregation and community.

If we pay attention to those persons who give so much of their life to the congregational program (like church school teachers and choir members) it will give new vigor to the entire congregation as well.

Very helpful in bringing the passive congregation to a new vitality is Lyle E. Schaller's *Activating the Passive Church, Diagnosis and Treatment*. In the chapter "Activating the Passive Church" is a check list for self-appraisal (page 66) which would be very beneficial to use in council meetings and at evangelism task force goal-setting meetings.

As new members are received into the congregation, help them move beyond a simple loyalty to an organization, the Christian congregation, to loyalty to the Christ. The means is discipling; the method is retreats, adult education courses, witness training, strong pastoral care and preaching on the stewardship of life. Regaining a deep sense of call through baptism for each person to carry out a ministry in the world is the result.

Congregational Witness Through
Reaching Out To The Inactive Member

A Prescription For Reactivation Of The Inactive

For a number of reasons, large numbers of our congregational members leave their active membership. Most often they just drift away. But sometimes a cluster of anxiety-producing events has caused them to leave. Many send out non-verbal signals to us that they are angry or anxious, or leave for a while to see if anybody notices, before finally dropping out. Primary to bringing a lost member back is an opportunity to ventilate the hurt which took place in their lives.

The Christian witness must therefore be a good listener when calling on members. How much better it is to discover the discontent before — not after — they leave. Often the real complaint is not the first one to be verbalized, so the listener must hear him or her through for the real grievance to surface.

Almost always this kind of person will send some primary signals to us that he or she is unhappy, whether it be an inward blaming of the self for the event or an outward blaming of the pastor or congregation. This discontent may manifest itself in a variance of worship attendance, activity on a committee, or side comments made to other members of the congregation. Or it simply may be done by stopping financial support to the church to see if anybody notices, or even more important, if anyone cares.

There must be much love and concern expressed by the congregational family for inactive members' absences. So often when the discontented send out the message they are unhappy, no one notices. As they perceive the absence of response, it is interpreted to mean no one cares if they're gone or hurt.

49

Inactive members certainly must have the experience of a visit in their home by the pastor, or better yet, by members of the congregation. They need special attention when returning to the church for pastoral acts such as marriage, burial of a family member or baptisms. A great dose of grace is needed for this to happen without deepening the guilt for their inactivity. All members have to sense that they are very important to the congregation, the pastor and the working committees.

An inclusive environment in the congregation will be necessary for an embarrassed inactive member to comfortably get back into an active role. The returning member ought to have a chance to worship without ridicule or sarcasm from the faithful. Occasions like Christmas and Easter, when social pressure might bring them back to their church, need to have a comfortable environment. It just won't do to have an usher who comments when the inactive person finally does return: "Well, Harry, the roof's going to fall in! You're back in church today!"

Keep those inactive members up-to-date by continuing to inform them well on the news and activities of the parish. When the church's guidelines demand we move them from the active to the inactive list, let's remember that this doesn't mean to drop them from our pastoral and congregational concern. Other thoughtful members of the congregation must continue to pray for them.

We ought to provide, in the life of our congregation, a number of opportunities for people to start over. Reunions of confirmation classes or new member classes, celebrations of anniversaries and other such events are logical times.

The pastor will continue to ask the inactive to help at the church, but in a very sensitive and gentle way so that the member can provide a good indication of where to serve and what that contribution will be.

We must be absolutely certain that the inactive members' suggestions for the congregation are heard, acted upon, and that this action is communicated back to them. A few people, having been treated in this fashion, will make their way back into the congregation if they can do it without losing face.

It is important to give the returning, inactive member an opportunity to take part in a membership training course which emphasizes discipleship. They often, for the first time, will feel an understanding of what it means to be a Christian and a member of this body of Christians, the congregation.

All the above says that reintegration into the fellowship as well as the membership of inactive members is a very important prescription for their inactivity to reverse. By all means, remove the red tape so that the reactivated can integrate into a more satisfactory and sensitive congregation than the one they left.

In considering our prescription for the inactive member, remember those basic doctrines of our Christian faith: the divine initiative, God's grace and love, the gift of baptism, the doctrine of being sinner and saint at the same time, and the atonement God has provided for all of God's people. A healthy understanding of the church as made up of sinners who need forgiveness and a fellowship of imperfect people results in a place where salvation is celebrated as important.

Some Preventive Measures

A primary way in which we can prevent members from becoming inactive is to be very intentional about integrating our new members into the fellowship as well as the membership. That fellowship includes those who are the "permission withholders," others who are called "pillars," and those whom we might consider the pastor's close friends — all of whom have the power of decision-making.

Good pre-membership instruction about discipling with a heavy emphasis on loyalty to Christ and Christ's church rather than loyalty to an individual congregation and/or pastor will be helpful, as is any measure which develops loyalty to Jesus Christ rather than a personality cult of the pastor. At that time we want to lay out careful expectations for new members as to constitutional requirements for remaining active.

Another preventive measure of inactivity is to give strong support to our members in whatever their work in the congregation might be. They should have an agreement as to how long they are expected to do the job, exactly what is expected of them, and how they can measure that expectation.

Sensitivity to members' hurts and personal life changes is critical. We must learn to read the indirect communication of disenfranchised members and give opportunity for all the membership to have their views expressed, heard and acted upon.

To appeal to various lifestyles and thus prevent inactivity by people who feel the church just isn't relevant anymore, there needs to be a variety of worship opportunities and formats.

Plenty of recognition for any contribution our members make to the ministry of the congregation and the ministry in their daily lives should be given as well.

Make sure there is openness in all business matters and decisions of the congregation.

Have a precise method of detecting members' changes in attendance and participation patterns so it is noticed when they are withdrawing. Structure as many crossroads for checkups as possible in the congregational life. By crossroads I mean those times when the church says it's now time to celebrate or observe a certain life experience such as first communion, confirmation, graduation, house blessing, the birth of a child or grandchild, or even the age when a child is ready to start church school.

We ought to make certain that every member of the congregation has a particular ministry and discipleship at which she or he works as a part of membership in the congregation within the first year. This means there ought to be reasonable, measurable expectations and completion dates.

Some Traps To Avoid

It is a mistake to use the same people and the same training for calling on prospective members as we do for inactive members. It is especially important in calling on the inactive that there be thorough debriefing and payoffs as a result of that very difficult work.

On the other hand, some congregations make the mistake of putting their whole evangelism effort and energy into trying to reach the inactive. While that is an admirable thing and needs to be done, it is probably the least productive work lay people and clergy can do in ministry. That doesn't mean it ought not be done; it just means there is very little result for the tremendous energy expended.

Let's be very careful about the trap of using "the letter" which is not personal and rarely effective in reaching inactive members. And probably the biggest trap of all is to talk loyalty to the congregation rather than to the Christ when we recruit members in the first place.

Congregational Witness Through
Integration Of New And Inactive Members

Congregations of believers and evangelical pastors have worked for years at doing intentional integration of new members into the fellowship. This seems so important to our whole ministry and congregational life. Perhaps one of the best ways we can get at this opportunity is to receive new members into the congregation halfway through the membership information class. The second part of the class, then, can emphasize to the new Christian what it means to carry out his or her own ministry in the world as well as through congregational efforts. Discipling of the new member during the second part of the class is one way some evangelical pastors have realized this responsibility (see Chapter 1). This means that all new members learn how to be stewards in the fullest significance of that word, and evangelists and witnesses as well.

Some congregations have found a sponsor system to be very helpful. When new members are received into the church, they are sponsored by members who are already not only in the membership but further into the significant fellowship of the congregation. For one year these people "shepherd" the new member and introduce them into the core group of Christians there.

When folks are received into the congregation, take their picture and publish or display it for the congregation. Hold a reception for them. There are many other ways that might be used to get the new member well acquainted and introduce them to the present membership.

Gift identification is very important in integrating new members and inactive members into the congregation. This means that we help each one of our new members identify how God has blessed him or her and in what ways personal ministry might use those gifts during the week, not only where they work, play and live, but also discover how those gifts might be used in carrying out the congregation's ministry.

Certainly every witnessing pastor and congregation will want to keep a good record of attendance at worship and the offering patterns of new members. After six months of attendance as a new member, a telephone call using a detailed checkup list from the volunteer or pastor, can be helpful in seeing how that person is integrating into the fellowship. Such questions can be asked as: Are you receiving the denomination's magazine in your home and reading it? Do you have a young person in your home who has started church school, confirmation or first communion? Have you discovered a way you can minister to the people you work with during the week? Have you developed some new friendships at your church over this last six months? A sample checkup that I have used is shown on page 55.

After one year of membership, hold a celebration for those people, giving special recognition at one of the worship services, then take them out to lunch to ask how it has gone during the first year of membership.

As discussed in the last chapter, we should structure as many religious crossroads or observances as possible in their lives so that the church approaches them as many times as possible to provide meaningful experiences.

SIX-MONTH CHECKUP FOR NEW MEMBERS

Name _____

Phone _____

Date received into (name of church) _____

1. Have you:
    ____ joined a choir (check on youth and bell choirs, too)?
    ____ Attended a church school class?
    ____ Joined a women of the church group?
    ____ Completed a discipling card?
    ____ Been called to serve in your area of interest?
    ____ Been receiving the church newsletter?

2. Are you a part of any of the following small groups? (Which?) (Caller should only ask about appropriate groups)
    ____ Singles of the parish
    ____ Married couples (which)
    ____ Fellowship for retirees
    ____ Thursday morning Bible study
    ____ Senior high youth
    ____ Junior high youth
    ____ Saturday morning fun — Kindergarten-Grade 3

3. Is there anyone at your house for: (only ask about appropriate groups)
    ____ First communion — Fifth graders
    ____ Youth choirs, youth bell choirs, other music programs
    ____ Confirmation program for seventh through ninth grades

4. Have you been able to:
    ____ Make new congregational friends?
    ____ Attend worship and communion regularly?
    ____ Share your faith with friends and neighbors?

5. Do you have suggestions for:
    ____ The worship service?
    ____ The staff and our ministry?
    ____ How we reach out to you?

Special remarks_____

_____

_____

Date of interview _____

In larger congregations where there are membership classes of considerable size, a steward from the group can be appointed to watch over the attendance patterns, giving patterns (regularity, not amounts), and general activity of the new member for the first year of membership.

Since most groups in a congregation lose the ability to assimilate new members into their fellowship after several years, frequent organization of new groups provides for a variety of interests and a repeated opportunity to join and develop close friendships within the congregation.

Perhaps the best way of all to integrate the new Christian into the congregation is to begin teaching them how to participate as the intentional witnesses and evangelists in the congregation. Immediately upon their joining, they can be recruited to carry out the evangelism calling on prospective members for the next six months. Remember that we ought to spend as much energy and budget on these new members immediately after they join as we did beforehand.

Small Group Organization

As mentioned, organizing new groups on a continual basis provides opportunities for developing friendships within the congregation. Most groups in a congregation lose the ability to assimilate new members into their fellowship after they are 18 months old which accentuates the need to form new groups frequently.

The church growth experts have told us that the following seven ratios are helpful in checking out just how we are doing in integrating the new members into our congregation (Arn #3).

1. *The role task ratio ought to be 60:100.* This idea says that there ought to be at least 60 jobs for every 100 members of our congregation. These can't be busy work but must be kingdom work, and they ought to focus on meeting needs and changing lives.

2. The group ratio ought to be 7:100. There should be at least seven groups for every 100 members of our congregations. When we have less than this, there is a high rate of inactive exiting through the "back door," the consequence of their not being able to build meaningful relationships.

3. The new group ratio ought to be 1:5. One of every five of our present organizational groups should have been started in the past two years! As mentioned earlier, groups reach a saturation point somewhere between nine and 18 months following their formation. They aren't effective after that in assimilating new members. If we can keep to this new group ratio it means we'll continue to provide opportunities for new members to be involved and feel included. The dramatic thing about this principle is that when we start new groups, we may have to find a way of stopping some old ones that are no longer useful.

4. The friendship ratio ought to be 1:7. Our new members should be able to identify at least seven new friends within our congregation within their first six months of membership. Those first six months are really important! New members who have not been integrated into the body of members the first six months are beginning to ease out the back door into inactivity.

5. The parish council ratio ought to be 1:5. Sometimes our constitutions will not allow it, but one of every five council members should have joined the congregation within the last two years. This also should hold true of all committees of the congregation. You see, in doing this, we encourage an openness in the power structure and we assure our membership of its real mission.

6. The visitor ratio ought to be 3:10. This would say that three of every 10 of our first-time visitors ought to be actively involved in the congregation within one year. National studies seem to indicate that churches are seeing four of every 10 local visitors come back a second time. Seventy to 75 percent of these will join within a year. Non-growing congregations see only five to 12 percent of their first-time visitors eventually joining.

7. *Staff ratio ought to be 1:150.* Church growth philosophy says that a growing church ought to have a full-time staff member for every 150 persons at worship. If the ratio reaches one to 225 or 250, it is unusual to see any significant increase in active membership.

While this church growth philosophy seems rather mechanical, the intentionality of specific attainable numbers can give us handles to present to the evangelism task force and the parish council. Changes can then be brought about that will make us more effective in reaching out to our inactive members and integrating new members so that they do not become inactive.

CHAPTER 3
Parish Area Witness

Area Witness Through The Media

The media available today offer us unique opportunities to share the gospel and invite non-church people into our fellowship. Selecting a radio station, for example, or the type of advertising best suited for our congregation can be a tricky business. Air time on the smaller stations and the "religious" stations is often less expensive, but these stations may not be heard by many of the people you're trying to reach.

Broadcasting the worship service over a 30- or 60-minute program of free time offered by a station will be of great benefit to the shut-ins of the congregation and those already converted to the Christian faith. However, those we would like to reach with the gospel, the unchurched, probably will not listen for 30 or 60 minutes at a time to the radio for instruction about their faith, let alone be converted.

Thirty seconds of crisp words during "drive time" is probably the best use of a congregation's money for radio advertising. This means that in the larger metropolitan areas the time frame in which the 30-second ads are offered would be morning and evening when people are driving to and returning from work. Most advertisers also believe it is better to purchase many 30-second ads over a week's period to saturate the market, rather than trying to put on an occasional one and hoping people catch it sooner or later.

Many U.S. congregations find that advertising in the newspaper is the most widely read and effective way of media advertising. This takes very intentional strategy to be done well and be effective. Practically all news organizations have more material than print paper to put it on, so they must be selective of what copy gets into the daily or weekly newspaper.

It is best to make a visit to the managing editor or to the religion editor of the local paper which goes into the homes of your prospective congregational members. Take along a list of activities which have recently happened in your congregation and others which are coming up and ask the editor which ones are newsworthy. From the response, you can get an idea of the type of article he or she would like to have submitted on a regular basis.

Be sure to find out from the editor what format is preferred, so that you know how to present your interesting material to make it handy for editors to include in their copy. Most newspapers prefer double-spaced copy, with the item beginning one-third of the way down on the first page, so that the empty space can be used for writing "heads." Write only on one side of an 8½- by 11-inch paper and be sure that you type it. The old rule of asking yourself, "who, what, when, where, why and what's interesting about it?" is still good. Be sure to include on the front page your name and phone number so that it is handy for a reporter to follow up on the story to get additional information.

Often a newspaper will have a page listing for church news each week and if you are willing to write up a brief story, it will get included some of the time. Remember that the name of the game is persistence. They pick and choose every week. Keep furnishing a weekly item and never complain if it does not get in.

Each newspaper will have a different photo policy, so be sure to discover it before you start taking pictures and submitting art for the newspaper. Smaller papers love to have photographs and have quite an appetite for them in each publication. A somewhat mediocre news item is bound to get printed if you provide good "art." This does not mean group pictures but individual action pictures which are in focus and in black and white glossy form. Adults should be consulted before their picture is used in any way. Be sure to get signed permission slips for any photos picturing people which you provide to the media. Parents of children pictured must sign for them.

Display ads are much more effective for churches if they are located somewhere other than the newspaper's church page. Display ads are often much cheaper purchased in local community papers, weekly papers and shoppers.

The Reverend Paul Lintern, who served three years as editor of the *Holmes County Farmer-Hub* in Millersburg, Ohio, before entering seminary, has written the following guidelines for the communications committee of one of Ohio's Lutheran synods:

> *"Although you certainly want to include the routine information about meetings and other events on an ongoing basis, look also for the unusual . . . people who are doing special or surprising things, a program that involves a certain type of person, anything that might be of interest to the average reader.*
>
> *"Be brief. (Journalists way, 'Write tight.') Pack all the facts into a couple of sentences, but be sure that they make sense as written. Ask someone to read it over for clarity.*
>
> *"Read the paper you are writing for and study its style, such as when to capitalize or use commas. Editors will appreciate that extra effort and likely be more gentle with your article.*

"Include as many names as appropriate. Submit stories about people doing things, rather than about things being done by people. Editors will generally be more pleased by this style.
"Respect deadlines."

Never — let me say it again — never complain to the editor of your newspaper about the treatment of your story. There isn't any way you can win with a newspaper. Continually submit the articles and, in the long run, you will have decent publicity through the newspaper.

Communities which have cable television available often have, by FCC regulations, what is called a "free access channel." This means that after a program is produced on three-fourths inch width television tape, placing it on the air is free. However, if you do not have your own equipment to produce such a program, you must pay for that production, which can be quite expensive.

Congregations can have provided to them, free of charge, over a public access channel, air time each week when they can furnish a station a purchased television program from the national church or other suppliers of such media materials.

Local television stations often look for "filler," background and news items during the festival seasons of the year such as Thanksgiving, Christmas and Easter. Try inviting them to film a portion of your worship service so that their reporting tells the community about celebrating that particular religious holiday. Remember, the television people are looking for the unusual and for the rather dramatic art.

Congregational Witness Through A Calling Program

Your new members are your best evangelists. Try inviting members you have recently received into the congregation to meet you for dinner at a local restaurant — the church should pick up the tab. After the meal together, some good fellowship, and devotions, ask the group to covenant with you to serve their church one Sunday a month for the next six months. This can be the basis for a calling group or "squad" which will meet regularly to call on prospective members.

When you get together for these sessions, try this schedule:

3:00 p.m. — Gather at the church for training

4:00 p.m. — Go out to make visits

5:30 p.m. — Have report session and meal at a restaurant

Assignment cards containing the names and addresses of prospective members will need to be prepared ahead of time. For the first few sessions it is important to send your fledgling callers out into easy witness situations, for instance, those who have regularly visited the congregational worship service in the last few months.

Each time the calling squad meets together for the hour training at the church, a different aspect of calling can be investigated and actually rehearsed by role playing. There are several resources for these sessions including a little book called *Handbook for Parish Callers,* the larger companion book, *Training Parish Callers,* and *Training Evangelism Callers: Caller Manual and Leader's Guide* (all are available from Augsburg/Fortress Press).

Remember that actual practice must take place in order to raise the comfort level of your people when making visits in the home. The calling squad members will learn at these training sessions how to tell of their own relationship with God to another person and develop good listening skills in order to hear the other person's story.

Two examples of group process which can be inspirational and instructional in these kinds of sessions are these:

Have your group divide up into pairs, with each partner not well known to each other, all in the same room, but separate from the others. Have the partners relate to each other their trip in detail to the church that day. Next, describe in detail their earliest remembrance of religion. Continue with telling the happiest time they can remember in practicing the faith, then their saddest moment. Finally, have each person

63

tell his or her spiritual trip from that earliest memory until the present day.

Taking the group through this process will last about 45 minutes and will be a very rewarding learning experience illustrating that every person has something to say as they listen and talk to another person about the faith.

The second group experience is similar. Repeating the same process, have them describe the kitchen table at home when they were growing. Second, share the saddest moments around that table, then the happiest moments around it. Now describe the altar at church. Next, share the saddest time around the altar. Last, have each relate the happiest time around that altar.

Your next step is to explain that the altar at our church is the table of the Lord, and we are family who have gathered to celebrate around that table, much like families and individuals who gather around tables in their own homes for celebrations, consultations and ironing out difficulties.

These simple exercises will help in putting your callers at ease in expressing their faith and showing them that everyone has a story to tell if we only listen.

High school youth like to do this sort of witnessing and witness training as well. Try having Saturday morning breakfast together, then the witness training before going out into the homes of prospective youth members and the youth of prospective adult members. A reporting session held after the visits is a very important part of the witnessing. Schedule these sessions on a monthly basis. Try calling them "The Youth Calling Squad."

Congregational Witnessing Through A Parochial School

Ms. Billie Navarro of the Division for Education of the Evangelical Lutheran Church in America has outlined nine good reasons in an article for *The Evangelizing Congregation* for having a parochial school and how that school can advance evangelism in that particular community.

First, Christian schools have a positive image for quality education, as she claims,

> *"Unchurched families account for 22 percent of the enrollment in pre-schools and elementary schools. The percentage of children from inactive families is also significant — even larger than unchurched (Navarro, 1)."*

This certainly tells us that the parochial school often can be that basic contact which will bring inactive and unchurched people to the congregation because of their strong desire for a good education for their children. They will do that even when they are disillusioned by the church or have incorrect perceptions about the vitality or relativity of the congregation.

Navarro also claims that children are often the best evangelists in their homes. We do know that young people repeat in the home setting what they have learned in the school setting. This means that the good parochial school can bring a positive communication of the gospel and God's presence in a family's home that would not otherwise even consider it.

Lutheran schools represent the entire diversity of the community, according to Navarro, since 26 percent of the children in the Lutheran elementary schools are children of color. This is a much better percentage than congregations in the Lutheran church have achieved to this date even in communities that are very mixed. The school is often the very best tool of God's spirit in establishing a contact with more recent members of the community when the congregational membership is mainly a reflection of these people who lived there a long time ago.

Navarro makes a very important point: that one of the most frequent reasons given for joining a Lutheran congregation has been for the sake of the children. It is an interesting fact that even children of "Baby Boomers" (those born between 1946 and 1964) and "Baby Busters" (the generation following the Baby Boomers) are brought to congregational ministries in order that they might "get a taste of religion." This means that the parochial school might be the very place where parents who are unchurched or inactive approach in order to see that their children have, oftimes for the wrong reason, this much desired taste of religion in their education.

Navarro says that parents are drawn back to the church when the children are enrolled in a congregation's educational program. This would, of course, depend on the creativity and aggressiveness any congregation uses in ministering to that which we call the "web" of the congregation. Church growth advocates often talk about the "extended" congregation. If a congregation sees its ministry as responsible for all those connected in any way to the membership of the congregation or involved in any of its programs, there is then a direct connection to the families, and even friends of the families, who bring their children for parochial education.

Navarro also tells us that when children are enrolled in a parochial school it gives a long-term contact by the congregation with the parents and those children. This is not just a one-time visit because somebody died or wanted to get married. Day after day, their children attend the parochial school and thus week after week the congregation has another opportunity to minister to their needs and bring them into the family of God.

Churches with preschools and day care centers attract families with young children. Of course, for the most part, parents of young children are often young adults — the very people that a congregation needs to attract in a given community. This is especially true in changing communities, and thus churches want very much to seek out those young adults who will become the movers and shakers of the community, and the producers of additional people in the community through their children for years to come.

It is interesting that Billie Navarro's paper claims that adult baptisms are higher in congregations that sponsor parochial schools. "Schools that report new member statistics average 10 to 30 new church members annually from school families (1)."

Those qualities which most urban neighborhoods feel they need, according to Navarro, are stability and quality education. To that statement we can add that the parochial school provides a spiritual dimension that is not allowed by law in the public schools. Of course, this is accomplished much better in some parochial schools than others, but certainly it is one of the great advantages of the congregation's having a parochial school where spirituality and Christian education are permitted and, indeed, can be creatively and aggressively pursued.

We have to measure very carefully the need and the possibilities for ministry in establishing a parochial school as a part of our congregation's ministry. If it will, indeed, sap away all the congregation's effort, energy and resources, then it may not be worthwhile. Or if it would remove all the Christian influence from the public schools by placing those students in our own parochial school, it might be in direct conflict with the scripture's admonition to be a salt and leaven to the whole lump. If it simply provides a way for parents to avoid their children's experience of a multicultural society and would thus feed bigotry and racism, then by all means we should not posture that sort of project in the name of the church of Jesus Christ.

On the other hand, Billie Navarro has provided for us compelling reasons to consider a parochial school that must be taken very seriously. Each community and congregation will need to evaluate the pluses and minuses and prayerfully decide for or against such an enterprise as a part of their ministry.

Congregational Witness Through Additional Worship Opportunities

"You can reach people you can't reach in the traditional 11 a.m. worship service, you can break your growth plateau, you can increase your income without increasing your expenses, you can boost your Sunday school attendance, you can add new cells, you can provide a different style of worship, you can establish your credibility as a leader (Towns, 2).'' So says Dr. Elmer Towns of the Church Growth Institute, noting reasons why he believes at least two worship services should be offered, even if space problems aren't a consideration.

It isn't difficult to figure out that when you add another service you double the capacity in the very same facility and you do it without increasing your expenses. Many congregations reach growth plateaus and thus adding another service will often help move beyond that plateau of 100 or 150 members. Towns contends that we would increase our income without increasing our expenses, but the truth of the matter is that to add another service does add some additional expenses.

Perhaps Towns' most important observation is that the homogeneous unit of church growth (which says that folks seek out groups similar to themselves to join and worship with) indicates that by adding another service we can develop yet another homogeneous unit which might be different from that at the original service. The two or three services on a weekend can then become homogeneous units of the one overall congregation.

All these reasons for having more than one worship experience seem to have some validity, but certainly the most important one to this author is that by adding another service we accommodate another or different group of people's lifestyle and worship needs. The Thursday night, Wednesday noon or Sunday night worship service — each appeals to a group of people for whom this different time for regular worship fits their weekly routine. It simply opens up and makes available worship opportunities to people for whom employment or other important routines conflict with the usual worship time slot.

Going to a second or third service certainly resolves space problems, since it can double our sanctuary capacity without remodeling or adding on. If you are in an urban setting where parking is crucial, remember that adding a second or third service increases by two or three times the number of cars that can be parked in the parking lot or the precious on-street parking around the building.

Church growth experts believe there is an "80 percent barrier." Towns describes that by saying, "When you are 80 percent full — you are full. Many people don't understand that a church will stop growing when it reaches 80 percent of its seating capacity (2)." If his premise is true, we have a compelling reason to continue to add services simply to accommodate a growth in numbers of people attending worship. I do believe that Towns is right when he advises, "If the only reason to add a service is to solve a space problem — don't do it (2)." How we go about establishing that next service is extremely important and how much of the congregation owns that decision is even more crucial.

Congregational Witness Through Reaching Secular People

Dean of Asbury Seminary's School of World Mission, Dr. George Hunter, notes 10 attitudes common in churches which consistently reach secular people and therefore experience growth (Arn, #33). These successful churches . . .

1. "*. . . know that people who aren't disciples are lost (1)*." Certainly there are various ways to interpret this, but at least we ought to say that we may have lost our urgency to do witness and outreach because we are not all that certain it makes a difference in life now and life hereafter. If we have a strong conviction that those who are unreached in this world miss a great joy in living here, and an even greater joy in eternity, certainly this will impact parish programs, priorities and the amount of energy, effectiveness and desire to witness to the unchurched in our communities.

2. "*. . . know that lost people matter to God (1)*." Hunter claims that "authentic evangelism flows from a mind that acknowledged the ultimate value of people (1)." One doesn't have to study the scripture or Jesus' parables for long to become

certain that the lost, forgotten and disenfranchised of our culture and society are very important to God and in need of God's love and forgiveness. This means that it is increasingly important that we reach out on God's behalf to these kinds of people.

3. "... *see their church as primarily a mission to lost people, rather than a gathered colony of the faithful* (1)." Hunter discerns beautifully the difference between maintenance and mission of a local congregation. We can do no less. One of the traps of a congregational ministry is that those already received into the congregation continue to demand that most of the congregation's pastoral and lay ministry efforts go toward meeting their needs. Yet the scriptures assure us that Jesus called not the righteous, but sinners, to repentance and claimed that a doctor comes to serve the sick and not the well. Moving a congregation to seeing its primary responsibility as witness and evangelism to the unchurched is one of the toughest ministries and yet the most exciting results come from it.

4. "... *have high expectations of their members* (2)." Many service organizations in the community demand far more of their members than any congregation would dare. And yet those congregations which seem to be experiencing rapid growth are those that expect great things from each person, especially soon after joining the congregation. Regular worship, generous stewardship, daily ministry by all the laity and witnessing to unchurched friends, neighbors and family members are simply expected of every member of the congregation. They assume that one has not reached full spiritual maturity or learned the great joy of being one of God's called our people until he or she has begun to live the Christian life with just such expectations being fulfilled.

5. "... *know what to change and what to preserve* (2)." Hunter writes, "In many plateaued and declining churches (and denominations) there is widespread confusion between what is 'form' and what is 'essence' (2)." Churches which have not experienced growth have probably operated in the same fashion for the last 40 years. They have had a desperate need for new

paradigms in the way they do ministry and witness but have resisted that in every direct and indirect method possible. Hunter tells us that congregations who are reaching the secular society and growing are ones that are very slow to change their theology but are very quick to adapt to cultural forms and styles which communicate what they believe.

There are some "sacred cows" about which one needs to be very careful moving or changing. Worship objects such as candlesticks, chalices, patens and so forth given by members are very important to some people and should not be disturbed unless there is a compelling reason to do so, and then only if careful preparations are made. Also make careful preparation to change flags in the chancel, methods of administering communion, times of the worship services, methods of ushering and those who do it, senior choir traditions, the placement of the altar. Very sensitive to change are former pastors now retired but still in the parish, choir directors or parish secretaries with a long tenure, older organized Sunday school classes or their longtime teachers and certain shut-ins like the former pastor or his or her spouse, Sunday school teachers of adults and monied people.

However, when it comes to the way in which we communicate the gospel and reach out to the community, the very latest of methodology can and ought to be employed.

6. ". . . *understand secular people* (2)." We must find ways to research, befriend and get to know better those secular people outside the organized church. This means being a part of groups where they are and encouraging our congregational members to develop personal relationships with the secular people of the world (no matter how scary it might seem!) by, as Hunter writes, "encouraging members to talk with non-Christians, spend time with them, ask them questions and make friends with them (2)."

7. ". . . *accept unchurched people* (2)." Of course we must always begin where people are, rather than insist they meet us where we are before we reach out or invite them into the kingdom. "The church is called to reflect God's own posture

toward sinners: acceptance and compassion. Often we Christians confuse acceptance with approval," writes Hunter (2). This is very difficult for an organized congregation which has been together for a period of time, likes each other and is very comfortable with each other's companionship. Congregations need to be challenged to accept those people who are not so acceptable to the rest of society. There is a real ministry in welcoming that person who has been invited by someone into the fellowship of believers. There will usually be strong resistance on the part of a few — or many — of the congregation to this radical concept of grace applied.

8. *". . . use music secular people understand (2)."* Most pastors of growing churches have concluded that their music is an even more significant factor in the church's outreach than the preaching! Since classical music accounts for only a minute portion of the album sales in the United States and contemporary music accounts for the rest, we should follow the lead of Martin Luther and Charles Wesley who reached people by using melodies from the local scene for contemporary music (of that time) to fit their theological words. We have to remember Hunter's advice that the music should be indigenous to the people these churches are trying to reach.

So, while it is true that we want to preserve the great German chorales — traditional music which has meant so much to us and with which we grew up as children — we also want to find those easily singable tunes in which our people can hear good theological words. Not only will they intellectually understand correct doctrine, but also "feel" in their hearts the joy of the message.

9. *". . . start new congregations (2)."* There are two great benefits to a congregation starting a preaching point and or another congregation. The first is that a new group of people who are primarily unchurched are reached with the gospel. In the ELCA, statistics reveal that sometimes up to 75 out of 100 people received into a new congregation as charter members are unchurched people.

In addition, the congregation which disciples the new church will find that an experience which is exciting and stimulating to the older congregation (not unlike other kinds of witnessing where the more one does it, the more one owns it). It is also true of congregations which witness by starting new churches.

10. *". . . are involved in world mission (2)."* Hunter claims that their concern for reaching people and conserving members extends beyond their own ministry area. Those congregations, who not only start local churches but also see their ministry as world-wide and provide for their congregational members a global perspective, will be the kind of congregations that secular people will seek out and join. We live in a global village and our culture demands just by virtue of watching the evening news and reading the daily newspaper that Christians take seriously the fact of world-wide community. Providing this broader view of evangelism and witnessing will make legitimate our desire to bring the gospel to the unchurched, even if it is of no direct benefit to the congregation where we serve and belong.

Why Baby Busters Don't Go To Church

Win Arn, in his publication, *Growth Report,* speaks of "Baby Busters." He defines them as "a group widely ignored in churches' outreach strategies. The nickname describes those young adults between the ages of 18 and 26 (the generation following the Baby Boomers [#33, p. 4])." In researching the Baby Busters, Arn lists the following attitudes which these folks seem to have toward the traditional church:

1. *They see it as boring.* These 18-to-26-year-olds simply do not perceive the church as involving them in planning for their age group in the worship experience. They also do not perceive our worship as having that joy, playfulness and deep sense of "other worldly" that they so desire. As a result, we must work at keeping our services moving and stimulating,

using the very best communication techniques to keep attention and to motivate.

2. *"They perceive it as irrelevant.* Arn claims that the Baby Busters simply perceive worship as a waste of time. They do not think the church addresses those struggles in which present day people are involved (#33, 4). Since we do have the good news of the scripture and can throw against that news such issues as abuse, addiction, loneliness, frustration, marital struggle, parenting and other painful issues of modern-day living, we have a relevancy which can penetrate right to the soul.

When Willie Nelson was awarded the country music award of the year, he was introduced as "the country singer whose music is always close to the ground." That kind of "close to the ground" preaching and teaching, along with enabling and discipling from the congregational members will, indeed, make that which we offer in our congregational setting relevant to the Baby Buster.

3. *They have other things they would rather be doing.* Arn says that time is one of the most treasured possessions of the Baby Buster. He goes on to claim that recreation, socializing and investment in one's own betterment receive a priority of any spare time available (33, 4). This means the competition is tough. It means we need to get priorities straight in programming our parishes for discipling our people, so they might gain new perspectives on the value of life's time itself. It certainly means that when we offer opportunities for spiritual growth they need to be meaningful, well-organized and obviously significant to the condition of life in the congregation and community and how it is doing right now.

4. *They feel that no one else attending church will be like them.* "Busters are looking for others like themselves for verification that there is something there worth going for," says Win Arn (#33, 4). So, we need to be intentional and evangelize that group of friends, relatives and family members in this significant age bracket. We need to have individuals taking part in the worship services, greeting, and so forth who demonstrate that Buster-age people there are deeply involved in the witnessing and worshipping ministry of the congregation.

Whether it be a Baby Boomer or Baby Buster, by involving each group in doing and planning the ministries of the congregation, we can fill their needs with integrity while still holding up before God's people the basic gospel, the creeds, confessions and catechisms which are the basic roots and traditions of our heritage.

Baby Boomers And Busters

"Baby Boomers don't like boring sermons, offering plates, coats and ties, or the narrow-minded Christianity many of them find in the average church," writes Jack Sims, a minister and an authority on the baby boom (The Des Moines *Register*). Sims' firm, BOOMERS Consulting, (Believers Outside Of Most Every Religious System) based in Placentia, California, specializes in helping clients understand Baby Boomers.

Sims claims that, "Baby Boomers go to church less than half as often as Americans over 40 do." According to Sims, ". . . dual wage-earner households use Sunday to do the laundry, shop and spend time with their family (The Des Moines *Register*)."

In his book *Why Are These People Smiling? Because They Don't Have To Go To Church Anymore,* Sims lists 10 traits of effective churches along with quotations from his interviews with Baby Boomers. Let's consider the implications for worship and witness practices and programs in our local parish in light of these suggestions. These are the 10 traits of effective churches:

1. *They will be open to experience.* In our hymn selection, worship liturgy and preaching, we must provide for the emotional "feeling" as well as academic and intellectual correctness. Passing the peace, social gatherings, greetings and other practices ought to provide opportunity to touch, embrace and experience, as well as be in exact compliance with the rubrics. Joy will need to be felt in the preaching and teaching, since "heart" is as important as "brain" in what we say and do

when God's people come together for worship. According to Sims, one Boomer said that going to church has to make him feel better.

2. *Teaching will stress practical living.* This generation seems to hunger for Bible study and preaching which deal with life's struggles where "the rubber hits the road." Retreats and classes in marriage enrichment, sermons on ethical and social issues of the day and the local community will be appreciated. God's help in relationships is important to the Boomers, and they want help with managing money and setting priorities for life.

In the popular television show, *Cheers*, Sam Malone tried to balance a number of girl friends in his life without having to marry any of them. Diane Chambers finally said to him, "You have to make some commitments and choices in life, Sam — It's called growing up." A Boomer put the same idea to Sims like this: "I don't want to hear about pie-in-the-sky. I've got to pay my bills and stay married."

3. *They will place a healthy emphasis on relationships.* In part, this means recognizing the significance in arranging our worship area so people can see each other's faces. It also means recognizing the importance of small fellowship groups and fellowship opportunities in connection with the congregation. Integration of new members into the congregation will need to very intentionally move the Boomers beyond the "membership" and into the "fellowship." Seeing, theologically, the sinner in a realistic fashion and learning how to establish and sustain a worthwhile relationship will be attractive to them. One person told Sims that he didn't like sitting in a pew for an hour and looking at the back of someone's head.

4. *They will share their faith by what they say and do.* Directly connected with the preaching and teaching of Jesus and his model of a radical love for the unlovely, this group will need plenty of opportunities to do that radical loving. Help for the poor and hungry, food pantries, day care centers, rescue missions and a variety of social ministry projects will be expected. As we talk about the priesthood of all believers, the

Boomers will expect to share in the leadership of the worship and be taught how to carry out their ministry in the world where they live, work and play each day. Sims reports one as saying, "It's important to me that a group's walk matches their talk."

5. *They will have fewer titles and less formality.* This will dramatically effect the way clergy will present themselves and the style of leadership which will be most effective and attractive. The distance between the pew and the pulpit should be shortened. Less formality, more simplicity and more lay participation seem to be indicated. "Our minister is not called reverend, doctor, father, pastor or brother; his name is Chuck."

6. *A congregation attractive to these Baby Boomers will understand the new family in America.* Our language in newsletters, bulletins and announcements will need to take into account that the average family is not mother, father, son and daughter. Our stewardship should not assume one wage earner per family or a man as head of a household. Youth programs will not even hint that children have both parents living at home with them, and sermon illustrations need to avoid the stereotypical description of traditional households. One quoted by Sims stated, "Our families are more like the 'Brady Bunch' or 'Kate & Allie' than 'Ward and June Cleaver.'

7. *They will recognize the ability of women.* We'll need to get rid of the cookie-baking, quilting and nursery-tending mentality for women. Our worship language must not be sexist. Second-rate citizenship for the women of the parish just won't do any more. If we are to reach this group, positions of power on governing bodies, including the finance committee, are imperative. Women need to be visible in worship leadership, administration and organization of the parish. In many cases scripture can be phrased to be less sexist and more inclusive without doing damage to its intent or divine inspiration. One woman said, "Working in the board room on Monday and the nursery on Sunday won't inspire modern women."

8. *They will place an emphasis on worship.* This age does want to experience God's presence in their lives. Worship will need to be done well, and preaching must be interesting, relevant and challenging. In order to accommodate the many different lifestyles in the community, the schedule of worship services must be more than one hour on Sunday morning. A healthy balance between "slave to rubrics" and "lone-ranger independence" must be struck. Variety and excitement and routine are all essential. It must be personal and corporate, equipping and interesting, instructive and inspirational. It ought to be fun! A Boomer remarked, "I want to get in touch with the supernatural."

9. *They will have a high tolerance for diversity.* Boomers will look for an alternative to our brothers and sisters of the so-called "evangelicals." Those of this generation do not want to check their brains at the church door. Most will not support bigotry and narrowness in any form. We must keep a strong emphasis on ecumenical relations and intelligent handling of interpretation of scripture. The Boomers will appreciate and expect an inclusive and diversified congregation as representatives of all God's creation — they have fought for civil rights and do not expect to see their congregation set those gains back inside the sanctuary.

10. *They will be action oriented.* Much movement and pageantry in the worship will be expected. "Doing" groups will be anticipated. Budgets will need to reflect a busy people of God on the move, and communicating the ministries of the nationwide expressions of the denomination — World Relief, Peace Ministries, Immigration Services and local social service agencies — will be important. The relationship between the local congregation and national and international causes and work will have eager ears. "Show me how I can make a difference" will be a prevailing attitude.

A brass plaque from a Mississippi river boat in the museum in Dubuque, Iowa, states, "In case of a storm, pray toward heaven, but row toward shore."

Remarked a Baby Boomer, "The Spirit of the Peace Corps is still alive."

Dolly Parton, Reggie Jackson, Cher and Sylvester Stallone — part of the 78 million nationwide Baby Boomers — all turned 40 in the 80s. Active politically, fed on excitement, and with better than a 50 percent divorce rate, these stereo-junkie, rock-and-roll, sexual revolutionaries with frisbees and running shoes want much more out of their churches than boring sermons absorbed by narrow-minded Christians in impersonal and cold church buildings.

Jack Sims claims they are yet reachable if we who are God's people will set the Spirit free in new and challenging ways. A congregation which takes seriously its commission and opportunity to share the good news and minister to "all people," including the Baby Boomers, will be one which will concentrate on experience, stress practical living and put a heavy emphasis on relationships. It will be informal, understand the new family, recognize the ability of women, place an emphasis on worship, have a high tolerance for diversity, and be action oriented. Its walk will match its talk.

Even if those dual-wage-earner households use Sundays to do the laundry and shop, there is still the possibility of an informal, action-oriented, inclusive Saturday night worship service. (See "Program Implications for the Effective Congregation" on pages 80-81.)

A Congregational Check List

The following check list provides ways to begin looking at what we are presently doing in the areas of evangelism and congregational outreach. These are ministries and opportunities for witnessing for which you'll want to provide the resources and people to accomplish:

1. Identifying and ministering, as well as witnessing to, the extended congregation. This is that group of five to seven people with whom each of our present members are acquainted and who live in our ministry area.

PROGRAM IMPLICATIONS FOR THE EFFECTIVE CONGREGATION

BABY BOOMERS	WORSHIP Emotional experience	WITNESS Sharing our story	STEWARDSHIP Supporting causes	EDUCATION Student-centered experiential learning	SOCIAL MINISTRY Hands-on service
1. Open to experience					
2. Practical living	Topical preaching on daily struggles	Survivors do witnessing	Help with money management	Courses on family living	Study of social issues
3. Emphasis on relationships	Personal & touch in worship	Integration of new members	Individual visits	Koinonia groups	Foster Grandparents Program
4. Walk-talk	Offerings for causes	Witness groups	Interpret budget in light of ministry. Lay ministry.	Consciencization of congregation	Volunteers for community organizations
5. Less formal	Informal worship 9 a.m.? Preaching partners	Witness where you live	Reword contribution statements	Education outside church building	Hold up other community work
6. New family	Singles, etc. as assisting ministers. Language in preaching and bulletins.	Target groups other than traditional family	Individual pledges	Classes for various citizens. Watch language and assumptions.	Promote and do references, etc. Sex education, widows, singles again.

7. Recognize women	Use women in worship. See women clergy as role models. Inclusive language.	Watch brochures.	Include on committees and in leadership	Study role of women	Support abused women and, rape victims, etc.
8. Emphasis on worship	Variety of services, interesting sermons	Invitation to worship. Television and radio advertising	Stewardship emphasis in worship	More worship education in community	Temple talks re: social ministries
9. Tolerance for diversity	Use of hymns and music. Minorities up front.	Go after minorities	Include in material	Study of minorities. Minorities teaching.	Cooperation with minority congregations
10. Action-oriented	Commissioning lay ministry	Calling groups	Support Designated Advanced Gifts	"Do" classes reflection on action groups. Enable to minister.	Advocacy groups. Hands-on experiences.

2. Communicating the gospel through the local media and public events. This means establishing the contacts and developing the expertise to make certain we are using all other avenues in communicating the gospel besides at the pulpit and through individual members.

3. Working hard at discovering all unchurched people within the service ministry area of our congregation.

4. Providing an opportunity for the preparation and training of witnesses and seeing that actual visitation to unchurched people takes place.

5. Providing opportunities for witnessing through serving ministries and that we are the instruments through which the gospel is being applied on community issues as well.

6. Placing witnessing and outreach as high priorities in ongoing congregational concerns such as educational programs, talks by lay people, stewardship programs, and other opportunities.

7. Identifying and cultivating our unresponsive and inactive members.

8. Seeing that spiritual lives are deepened by Bible study, meaningful devotional life at home and at church, and instruction and motivation for prayer.

9. Equipping each disciple of the congregation to know how to witness through the small group experience. This means holding retreats and Bible studies, organizing small groups around an issue or need, and permeating the parish with a strong emphasis on ministry of the laity.

CHAPTER 4
Multicultural Witness

Multicultural Witness Through Congregational Climate

Paul claims in Galatians 3:28: "So there is no difference between Jews and Gentiles, between slaves and free people, between men and women; you are all one in union with Christ Jesus (TEV)." But it doesn't always look like it!

We now live and minister in an age of many cultures living and working side by side. There is globalization of transportation, education and communication. In addition, we who have been called to witness are also called to set a climate for inclusiveness so that our congregations may better represent the full richness God intended in creating us as many ethnic groupings, speakers of many languages and many colors of skin. It is a reclamation of the multicultural church of the apostles, described in the New Testament.

Let's have a person on our evangelism task force who is willing to see to it that the congregation is first motivated and then programmed to foster a climate for inclusiveness. This

83

means that any announcements at the worship service or in the parish newsletter should include singles, widowed, divorced, as well as single-parent families. We just cannot assume any longer that our members exemplify any particular lifestyle in extending invitations. We need to avoid gender-biased language in the bulletin and printed material as well. The Evangelical Lutheran Church in America's *Guidelines for Inclusive Language* is a useful resource for this.

Nominees for the parish council and committees of the congregation ought to include as many women as men. Also, don't forget representation of various ages. If we have people of color and primary language other than English in our membership, they, too, should be placed in nomination for church council election.

Posters or art work in our church building should represent, as much as possible, various races, genders, ages and physical abilities — especially those minorities which are part of the congregation and are in the nearby community. Of course, persons of both genders and all ages should be recruited to serve as worship assistants (acolytes, ushers, altar guild, greeters, lectors or communion servers).

Of vital importance is making certain that the printed order for worship in the bulletin is easy to read and understand for those worshiping in the congregation for the first time; for example, those Latin words often used in liturgical and more traditional churches which are strange and meaningless for a visitor can be omitted or changed to their common equivalents. Some congregations improve upon this principle by printing the entire liturgy each week in the worship bulletin so that the newcomer can easily follow it.

The illustrations and contemporary stories we use during the preaching ought to be by authors of various backgrounds to which all people can relate. Let's talk about Martin Luther King Jr., Mother Teresa, Bishop TuTu, and people of color and primary language other than English in our neighborhood. Take note of the cultural holidays observed by people who are not of your color or ethnic background.

In selecting hymns for our worship service, represent various backgrounds. Interesting short stories about the hymns and hymn writers may be related before worship begins — especially for unfamiliar hymns. Commemorative days also offer a unique opportunity to tell the faith stories of women and men from various times and places. (For Lutherans, *The Hymnal Companion to the LBW* by Stulken, and *Festivals and Commemorations* by Pfatteicher are rich resources.)

While it is very difficult to change choir anthems to inclusive language, we ought to try to accomplish that whenever possible. Here are some suggestions for gradually moving to inclusive language.

The lessons can be read from a variety of reliable translations, selected for clear and easy understanding, inclusive to all those who hear it. The prayer of the church should include the petitions for the conditions of circumstances of women, men and children of various races, religions, nationalities and ages.

An intentional climate of hospitality will invite people from the surrounding neighborhood into the congregational activities and will include people of all racial, ethnic and religious backgrounds, all genders, ages and abilities in the life of the congregation. Vacation Bible School is perhaps the best program to get started in this emphasis. Church school follows close behind. Special social events and programs are also good times to carry out this idea of outreach to other than our own culture.

When having congregational meals and receptions, include foods traditional to members of the various backgrounds and ethnic groupings within your neighborhood or congregational outreach.

We must make every effort to be certain that our church facilities (parking ramps, wash rooms, nurseries) are accessible to the physically challenged. Certainly community groups which promote justice and fairness for all people ought to be joined and/or supported by the congregation and the parish pastor. The church building can be offered as a meeting place for these highly motivated people who are only occasionally well-connected to Christian congregations. Coalitions for the homeless, the hungry and other community groupings are good opportunities for the pastor and her or his congregational members to be seen and believed.

Assist all of your church school staff, those who teach confirmation classes, and those who lead church organizations in their leadership and teaching roles to be inclusive of various family styles, gender, race, age and different physical and mental abilities.

There are a number of ways which have been listed above that will get us started on being an intentionally inclusive congregation even before we are able to bring people who are minorities in our community into the fellowship of believers.

Multicultural Witness Through Inclusive Language

About the easiest place to begin easing into inclusive language is with your own patterns in speaking, preaching and prayers; be aware of the writing and wording of worship bulletin announcements, newsletter copy and reports. There is no need to make an announcement about the change — don't make a big deal out of it — just start easing into it. Drawing special attention to it may leave you open to those who like to complain at any little change.

In preaching you can use female images as well as male, women as illustrations of people around Jesus, and include minority heroes and heroines as well as majority.

Quote the young's special people, then ease from man into mankind and then into humankind; later add sisters to brothers and mothers to fathers when appropriate. Change metaphors like king and father to ruler and parent; change male pronouns for God to "God's" or "Creator's," then, try using "she" in reference to the Holy Spirit.

Be careful in the retranslation of scripture. Brother or brethren can be changed to "and sister" or "Christians."

When appropriate grammatically, change the pronoun "he" to "he or she." Change male pronouns for God to "God," "Holy Parent," "Creator," "Jaweh." Male images for God like "Father" can become "Parent" or "God," "King" become "Ruler," and "Lord," "Sovereign."

Some warnings are appropriate here — it doesn't work to try to change words to familiar hymns (select other inclusive hymns). Also remember that the more something is memorized by rote, the more difficult it is to change. Don't even try to change the Disciples' Prayer, the Creeds or the Trinitarian formula. Neither is it wise to change anything when it is in front of the congregation in printed form, like the lessons for the day printed in the bulletin. Remember that Jesus was a man. His pronouns should not be changed to be inclusive.

Here is some advice to keep in mind:

a. Admit your struggle and ask for prayers of the people.

b. Let men take the lead if any explanation is demanded.

c. Refer to the Holy Spirit as "her" — it's fun and she will bless you in your efforts.

d. Read the church's bulletin on inclusive language use. It really helps.

CHAPTER 5
Pastoral Witness

The Pastor's Witness
Through Example And Spiritual Wellness

The Christian pastor is confident of the call by God to ordained ministry of Word and sacrament and witness. The lay person baptized into the faith is also convinced that God has called through baptism to do ministry in the world wherever she or he works, plays and lives.

Many in the congregation will be looking to us as pastors to lead the way in living a lifestyle which celebrates our call to witness to God's grace, forgiveness and presence with us now as well as salvation and eternal life.

Our lives will need to set the example of invitation to the unchurched. We need not be apologetic in tactfully finding out the relationship with God, or lack of it, of people with whom we come in contact. It's easy to not witness or show any concern about the other person's relationship to God, excusing it by saying we don't want to be "obnoxious" in our witnessing. But Christianity ought to be caught like the measles! There needs to be a "holy infection" in the way we go about living our own lives and our own relationship to God that other people will catch from us.

Redeveloping a deep sense of our own call to be a witnessing pastor and people will be indeed helpful. The way we live out that call and take care of our own spiritual life will set an example and be attractive to others outside the faith.

We must all, pastor and lay, have an intentionality about how we care for our spiritual wellness. Here are some suggestions to incorporate into your life:

1. A daily scheduled period of uninterrupted meditation and prayer for at least a half hour (this may have to be longer if we face a more stressful day).

2. Regular worship experiences when we aggressively worship, pray, listen, sing and rejoice.

3. Participation in the loving fellowship of Christians where we contribute, as well as receive, as a part of the group.

4. Taking part in confession, absolution and reception of holy communion at least twice a month, and even better once a week.

5. Developing a keen awareness of the presence of God with us all day long. It may take some reminders, for a while, like written notes to ourselves.

6. A quiet few moments of prayer of thanksgiving before every meal.

7. Some sort of guided study of scripture each week, sharing with other Christians our struggles and joys in keeping the faith.

8. A few brief moments of saying "thanks" to God on our knees by our bed at the end of the day.

9. At least once a month, celebrating with other Christians something nice and good in our lives.

10. Once each week, giving ourselves in a special way for someone else who needs our support and God's love shared through us.

When we work at the above spiritual fitness, the principle Jesus taught us is true: "For to every person who has something, even more will be given, and he or she will have more than enough . . . (Matthew 15:29 TEV)."

For pastors, we could add to the above list:

1. Plan a time each month when we hear the word proclaimed and receive holy communion from someone else (when we are not in charge).

2. Locate our own pastor/confessor. Someone who cares about our spiritual health and nurture and who doesn't have anything to do with our career.

3. Schedule a time away from the parish at least two weeks in duration for study and relaxation.

4. Provide once a week fun with the family — not church-related — full of play and laughter.

5. Include quality time with our spouse and children or grandchildren or a significant other.

There is a special joy awaiting those pastors who celebrate as called pastors throughout all their ministerial life. Among all the other church rites, responsibilities, worship services and personal experiences, one of the most fulfilling and enriching is when we can see God's Spirit convince another person of the great privilege of being one of the baptized of God and called to be a disciple and witness in the kingdom work.

Pastoral Witness Through Preaching

Martin Luther wrote in his *Small Catechism* that the meaning of the third article of the Apostles' Creed meant: "I believe that I cannot by my own understanding or effort believe in Jesus Christ, my Lord, or come to Him; but the Holy Spirit has called me through the Gospel (Article 3, p. 14)." So we, who are called to witness, proclaim while the Holy Spirit calls others through our preaching of that good gospel.

We must therefore ask ourselves some penetrating questions about our proclamation: Are we making the call clear in our preaching? Are we making that call of the Holy Spirit interesting and inviting? Are we using our own gifts of the Spirit in the best possible fashion in the pulpit? Are we creatively using all the avenues open to us to proclaim the gospel?

Here are 16 suggestions for making our proclamation of the gospel as clear and inspirational as possible:

1. *Express the message as "good" news.* It's very easy to scold from the pulpit. However, in a day when self-esteem is low and self-worth is questioned, our message needs to build up people and to present Christ as a help. We can tell our listeners that they have security in their practice of Christianity and that they are safe here and in eternity.

The law points out our need for the gospel, but law ought to be used sparingly. Don't forget God's grace! We must not forget to find gospel, the good news element, in all that we address from the pulpit.

There is a danger in what we call "triumphalism," which means that we simply talk about getting our soul saved for eternity and that "everything will be all right for us who believe." Because of a fear of this emphasis, we sometimes err in never bringing up those promises which are comforting and reassuring. We Christians are the community of the saved and do have glory from the cross to share.

The "theology of the cross" is also hope-filled. When one beggar tells another beggar where to find food, it is with great delight that he/she tells of the nourishment and the discovery.

From the pulpit we have the privilege of affirming God's presence in the midst of the shambles of the lives of those who are gathered there.

Some televangelists hold up for us a tantalizing ideal of positive thinking and smooth, thin, watered-down stuff which is far from the New Testament gospel. Still they have something we need to see as well. It is a message for present hope and a good news which assures, lifts up and encourages.

Consider the beatitudes of Jesus in Matthew 5. Some scholars think that these are his sermon themes. For the most part, they are congratulations on "how it is for a Christian now." So keep the message of the good news.

2. *Share yourself*. The word share is overused, but it describes best what we ought to be doing from the pulpit. People who listen to the proclamation of the gospel need to see the proclaimer as human and warm, struggling with them, and called to witness.

As we write our sermons, we need to preach to ourselves, as well as the congregation. These messages will often be our most effective proclamations. (If you always have wondered why rich people seem to get God's blessings and not you, say that, examine it and let God's word guide you and your listeners.)

Be absolutely certain that your congregation has heard your "God" story. Older clergy were taught in seminary that they should never use the "I" or relate their own life experiences. Still, when we look at the biblical heroes, we find that they are willing to tell of their own experiences in order to instruct and inspire others.

Your congregation can relate to your spiritual struggles and will be especially interested about the way God has called you into your particular ministry and relationship with God.

3. *Be sure to announce the whole story — the heart of the good news.* Preaching can sound very fragmented by using the church year calendar when we follow the lectionary. Try to place the text of your sermon in the larger plan of God to save us. After all, preaching is often re-announcing what we have heard many times before. But a person might have to attend church every Sunday for a full year in order to get the full gospel story of what God has done for us.

In many of our congregations the cross, resurruction and Spirit-with-us must be proclaimed every Sunday. A visitor may attend just one time and the preacher's chance to witness sinks or swims by that particular proclamation.

Try occasionally giving a rather topical sermon, something like "From Moses to Mother Teresa in 20 Minutes," in which you give a summary of the Christian faith. However, guard against that proclamation's being so narrow and fragmented that it loses its significance for the first-time hearer or for those who are just beginning to mature in the faith.

4. *Be Bible obvious but not Bible idolatrous.* Textual preaching is essential and the people in our pews are hungry for it. A large segment of the congregational membership coming to our churches for worship want to hear the Bible used even though it's not always for a good reason.

The scripture is what makes us unique and different: Christians are distinctive people. People flock to the pulpit where the Bible is central. Evangelist Billy Graham has set a good example for us of visually demonstrating from whence he reads as he holds that Bible up in front of himself. In some congregations the worshipers can only guess what is on the pulpit desk: perhaps some distant typewritten manuscript. Try holding the Bible in your hands in sight of the congregation and reading the text from it. You'll find that this is a reassuring visual aid and will be appreciated by the laity.

5. *Preach from commitment for commitment.* Often we are tempted to exclude from our sermon the "so what?" We need to ask for an obvious change in response to our preaching. We need to be certain that we extend an invitation for people to take some action because of the good news they have heard.

Answer the questions "What does this truth have to do with me now?" "How should my work, play, life, daily ministry and congregational activity be effected by the truth which is proclaimed today from the pulpit?"

Remember that all who are seated in the pews may not be converted Christians. Explain the next step to take in order to move toward membership in the fellowship of believers and discipleship of Christ.

6. *Make the message inclusive.* Be sure, when "driving the message home" and describing what action needs to be taken because of this gospel, that you include all ages, sexes and persons of color and other ethnic backgrounds. Use heroes and heroines from other ethnic groupings and cultures as your examples.

This is also an opportunity for us to remove all sexist language from our vocabulary. It can be done gradually over a period of time and will be stimulating to the hearers of your proclamation (see the chapter, "Multicultural Witness Through Inclusive Language").

Confess your concern about the congregation's make-up if it does not reflect the neighborhood. Don't scold. Love the people and confess your own frustration at trying to accomplish inclusiveness by making the congregation reflect the full richness of God's creation. Coax, encourage, love — and let the Spirit enlighten.

7. *Keep it simple.* The founder of the Grand Ol' Opry coached those who performed there to "keep it close to the ground, boys." In introducing singer Willie Nelson at the *Country Music Awards,* the host said that Willie composed and sang his music "close to the ground." Just as Willie sings simply of life's everyday occurrences, we need to proclaim our gospel "close to the ground" as well. Much of our preaching, if it's to be close to the ground, will come from our experiences in giving pastoral care while making home visits and hospital calls the week before. Remove the theological words that only a few can comprehend. In our proclamation, let's learn to use narratives which can be told easily and retold without reading from our notes.

And please have a focus to what we proclaim. There should be an easily remembered theme which runs through the entire message. Although it should be in contemporary language, it should not be faddish.

If you can find a related object which can be held up for your listeners to see, it will provide additional focus and stimulate our ability to remember what has been said.

8. *Let it be well illustrated.* Be sure that you use "windows" in the sermon such as stories, anecdotes and good humor which will portray the great truths you want to proclaim. Have more examples ready than you'll need so that they can be used when you feel the need for more illustrative material.

Let the examples be yours! Carry a note pad with you year around to write down things as you see them happen. Try to keep away from the books of illustrations which often use the life of Napoleon, Lincoln and Joan of Arc! It's better to use your daily newspapers and news magazines which are full of stories illustrative of the struggles which we humans face. Develop a file of these under general headings. There is a good reason for knowing the theme and text of the day ahead of time: so that incidents will ring a bell as you observe them. Be sure to watch television, see contemporary movies, go to sports events and generally live close to the ground, as your congregation does, so that your illustrative material is real and meaningful to them.

9. *Tell the people ahead of time what to prepare for in the proclamation.* Often an introduction to the sermon theme and a brief outline can be included in the worship bulletin. If you have a weekly newsletter, an item can be placed there, as well, under the title, "Get Ready for Worship."

Use banners, inserts and children's sermons to help drive home this focus of the day.

A congregation will be very appreciative if you will step out into the sanctuary before the worship service begins and briefly describe the theme for the worship service and what you'll be trying to accomplish in the sermon. You may want to point out in the lessons, prayers and hymn of the day how that theme is further revealed.

The anticipation of following this theme adds a great deal in making communication effective as you actually do it.

10. *Keep it short.* Our present generation has been brought up on 14- to 15-minute segments on television and are conditioned to short attention requirements. I doubt if it is productive to preach, no matter how eloquent we are, more than 18 minutes — 15 is probably better. If we do go for the longer sermon, we must make absolutely certain that we have a change of pace in order to attack the message in a different fashion to give variety and accommodate the short attention span of these folks to whom we proclaim in our day.

A four- or five-minute children's sermon using a good visual aid and a 15-minute adult sermon on the same theme will do more than 20 minutes of theological eloquence!

However, it probably is true that children's sermons which are most effective are usually given by people for whom that comes very naturally. If that's not your thing to do, you probably shouldn't try!

11. *Involve lay people in proclamation and evaluation.* Several times a year be sure to ask your congregation what subjects they would like dealt with from the pulpit.

Ask the worship committee to help with sermon planning by providing a worship survey. Be sure to ask people who are not attending church as well as those who are regularly present each week.

Many congregations find it valuable to have a discussion of the sermon immediately after the service in some kind of informal format, perhaps over coffee.

"People sermons," which your parishioners help to prepare, are well received by congregations. Ask seven or eight members of the congregation from various backgrounds, cultures and ages to come together with you on a Tuesday night to study the scripture for the following Sunday and share their ideas of what God would like to have proclaimed from the pulpit because of what that scripture says. Write down as many of their comments as possible. Then, as you work at preparing your sermon during the rest of the week, make a conscious effort to quote these folks by name (if you have their permission) in the sermon itself. You will find this an exciting way to communicate the message and downright fun for the people who help you, those who hear you, and yourself. Don't neglect to get together with the assisting group for Sunday lunch and talk about how it went.

Using preaching partners is another good way to stimulate the proclamation of the gospel. Enlist six people for six months who will fill out an information sheet each week concerning their thoughts about the scripture and return the ideas to the church by the Tuesday or Wednesday previous to your preaching the sermon. This paper, as illustrated, can ask the preaching partner to give a number of suggestions.

PREACHING PARTNERS HELP

For Sunday: _____ Date: _____

Gospel: _____ Or Lesson: _____

Here is how the text affects me: _____

_____

_____

Questions I would like answered about this scripture: _____

_____

_____

Here is what I think God would want said to our congregation Sunday: _____

_____

_____

Illustrations I think of: _____

_____

Ideas from my journal: _____

_____

Newspaper, television, movie, magazine ideas: _____

_____

Some ideas I suggest for our church because of this gospel:

_____

_____

Signed: _____

    Your Preaching Partner

Return to the pastor before noon each Wednesday.

12. *Get excited and have enthusiasm.* It seems to me that people "catch the gospel" like they catch the measles rather than intellectually internalizing it. If our rescue is that great and the news is that grand, why not let it become contagious in our presentation?

If that is true, then the preacher cannot be bound to a manuscript or always fenced in with a pulpit. Let the hands be free for meaningful gestures! Diligently guard against that holy "stained glass voice" which often invades our speech when we get inside that pulpit.

It helps to keep a critic watching you for "word whiskers," "verbal pauses" and mannerisms which individual members of the congregation will notice but will not tell you.

Most dynamic preachers claim that they cannot deliver a good sermon unless it has been practiced out loud ahead of time! The same is also true of reading the scripture in a meaningful fashion.

13. *Vary it — change the way it's presented.* It is just not reasonable any longer to give "three points and a poem" and call it stimulating proclamation. Our competition with electronic communication is real: it is professional, effective and to the point.

As a result, we need to find as many ways to vary the proclamation as possible. The following is a list of some variations which can be considered: sermon dramas, teaching sermons, dialogue sermons, Bible studies, several voices reading scripture, "people" sermons, use of visual aids, outline of the sermon in the bulletin, a sermon series on a common theme, a hymn in the middle or lay people offering several prayers throughout the sermon.

14. *Deal with issues of the day.* Although some pastors are fearful of dealing with controversial issues, this type of sermon subject doesn't need to offend, and we should not be afraid to take on the tough issues that everyone is thinking about anyway.

If the preacher holds up the general biblical truths alongside the problem and admits that he or she, too, struggles and is even frightened to present it to the congregation, it helps the listeners to identify with the struggle and think more about the issue itself. You must avoid presenting the social justice implications of the gospel in such a fashion that individuals think you are saying that those who don't agree with you are going to hell.

We haven't accomplished anything constructive if we drive away those people whose minds need to be opened for inspiration and change. Instead, they must be called to discipleship through our proclamation.

A congregation will respect the preacher who does not scold but coaxes, encourages and stimulates further discussion.

15. *Be sure to talk about money.* Money is what Americans understand best. It directs our lives. How we get it, what we do with it, and how we give it away are very big issues and often set all the rest of our priorities.

To be relevant we must talk about our cash, credit cards, savings accounts, charge accounts and checkbooks. In this country a person's checkbook is still the best indicator of who that person is and what he or she worships. Certainly we have missed touching a large part of our parishioners' lives if we ignore the subject of money.

16. *Take seriously the Holy Spirit.* While this is last in the list, it is by far the most important! So much of the rest of the worship is cut and dried, in print and predictable. But during these 15 minutes of preaching, we can allow for the surprises, mystery and playfulness — the serendipity — to take place.

All week get the text in mind and let yourself be inspired by God's Spirit. Remember over and over your call to be a witness. Allow the text to direct your own life as well. Then pray before you go into that pulpit — and lay yourself open so that God can come into you and surprise even you. By the time you get into the pulpit, if properly prepared, preaching will be from the overflow.

Never apologize by saying, "I'm no theologian" or "I'm not a great preacher." It's God's good news we bear. It's

God's Spirit that is aching to be set free through us. We are called to do this. And the God who calls us also provides the inspiration to do it effectively.

Prayer is the center. We preachers need to take seriously our beliefs about that Spirit and learn how to open up our lives to her so that she can speak through us.

Let's remind ourselves as we approach the pulpit, "I cannot by my own understanding or effort believe in Jesus Christ, my Lord, or come to Him; but the Holy Spirit has called me through the gospel (Luther, p. 14)."

Pastoral Witness Through
Six Troubles Turned To Opportunities

While in Tucson, Arizona, where I was conducting a field seminary at Our Saviour's Lutheran Church, I walked down Speedway Avenue and stopped at Miller's Curio Shop to see what I might find as a souvenir from the Southwest.

I found there a $1.50 treasure! It is a little reed container, painted yellow, which has six tiny dolls inside. The instructions for using the dolls state that in the land of Guatemala, the Indians tell this old story: When you have troubles, share them with your dolls. Remove one doll from the basket for each problem before you go to sleep and tell the doll your trouble. While you are sleeping, the dolls will try to solve your troubles. And since there are only six dolls, you are allowed only six troubles a day!

I'd like to pose for you six troubles we Christians who are called to witness can hand to our trouble dolls and overnight be made into possibilities for God's people.

1. *America is a mission field.*

The trouble is, we Americans think of ourselves as being churched Christians and send missionaries to other countries, but America itself is a mission field as well.

2. *Our congregations should be vital mission stations from which God's disciples and witnesses go out into the*

neighborhood and homes where we work, play and witness.

The trouble is, 80 to 85 percent of all congregations in the United States are in a state of decline or passivity. We need to find a way to breathe new life into congregational dry bones like Ezekiel describes in the Old Testament story.

3. *Our faith in Christ ought to lead us to be inclusive, welcoming, caring, loving people of God.*

Trouble is, the way we worship and the way we organize our congregations often leads us to be just the opposite. As the Berlin Wall came down, so walls that separate us in our communities and parishes need to come down.

4. *We have the potential to offer the Baby Boomers turning 40 a vital religious faith for which they are searching.*

Trouble is, we have dismissed them as hopeless and unreachable. We need to find ways to communicate to these middle-aged people and their younger counterparts, the "Busters," God's good news and a meaningful lifestyle.

5. *A wave of older Americans is hitting the population right now in the United States.*

John Naisbitt, futurist and author of *Megatrends*, calls the coming age wave **the most important trend of our times**. Trouble is, we haven't begun to tap this older citizenship as a vital element of discipling, witnessing and ministry.

6. *Each of our present membership has, on an average, five to seven friends, acquaintances or family members who are unchurched.*

Trouble is, we haven't begun to program our parish or order our ministry to this extended congregation where the real possibilities are. This "extended congregation," so called by our sisters and brothers in the church growth movement, is our best place to evangelize, with by far the most potential for new members.

In a recent article in *The Evangelizing Congregation,* published by the Division for Congregational Life of the ELCA, we find that 44 percent of all American adults were unchurched in 1988 (ELCA). Furthermore, 72 percent of the unchurched say they believe Jesus is God, or the son of God. In 1988, "58 percent of the unchurched say they would definitely, probably or possibly, return to church" (ELCA). Further, we learn that only one in three Americans was invited to become involved in a church over the past year, but about half of these who were say they responded favorably (ELCA). By careful affirmation of witnessing and teaching witnessing skills at the parish level, we can turn this "trouble" into a magnificent opportunity.

One of those dolls will have to work on how to move passive congregations to active, vital mission stations for the kingdom. Lyle Schaller, in his book titled, *Activating the Passive Church,* tells us that the most common reason for passive congregations is "the sense of mission being eroded and replaced by a priority on institutional self-preservation (1, 2)." He claims that "orientation toward today and tomorrow gradually becomes replaced with the past (52)." He points out other danger signals, like building a satisfying ministry around paid staff and the departure of the long-tenured pastor from a minister-centered church. Others explain that a congregation loses its vitality and reason for being around the 40th or 50th year of its life, unless some very intentional, strategic planning is done to avoid this decline or passivity (Arn, #3). We can do that, and the trouble doll can turn the passive congregation into an evangelizing community.

We do have a problem, particularly with congregations who take great pride in their ethnic background or who build walls around the congregation and certain ethnic groupings. This exclusiveness keeps us from realizing the full richness of representing God's creation of all sorts and kinds of human beings.

Walls must be broken down around the holy aura on Sunday morning as the only time when we can worship.

They need to be broken down between the insiders, who know their way around the building and through the complicated liturgy, and the outsiders, who are unfamiliar with it.

They need to be broken down between the clergy and laity, between the chancel and the pew, between races, sexes and nationalities.

Walls have to come down around the assumed traditional family, so that the single person, parent and children of divorce might be included as well. The walls between generations have to be flattened, as do denominational walls.

The Baby Boomers are turning 40 now, as we saw in Chapter 3, and have very specific expectations of their church in their search for Christian faith. Read again in Chapter 3 for specifics.

Let me here briefly review: They want so much to be part of a congregation which is open to experiencing things with the heart, as well as with the mind. The Boomers want help with practical living, such as staying married and paying the bills. They want a strong emphasis on building relationships with other human beings, and how to maintain them or make them even richer.

They'd like to see our walk equal to our talk. That is, the Boomers want to be active and follow the direction and counsel of the scripture. Along with a lot less formality in the worship experience and the pastoral leadership, the Boomers want recognition of the new family, which isn't necessarily comprised of 2.5 children, a mother and a father living in the same house. They want women to receive full status with men in the parish, and the possibility of reaching their full creative potential.

They'd like an emphasis on worship and getting in touch with the supernatural, and see tolerance for diversity. What a challenge to organize the parish to meet their needs with what we can offer as God's people called to witness!

Certainly the church can find challenge and opportunity in an aging America. In 1985, for the first time, the number of people in the U.S. over 65 exceeds those under 18 (Arn #26, p. 1). This author is now a part of that segment of society 55 years and older, which is multiplying three times faster than the population at large. As noted in his church growth newsletter, Win Arn's research suggests that this age group "indicate they desire a more vital and meaningful Christian faith (#26, p. 3)." It also states that "senior adults as a whole are particularly receptive it the gospel and its relevance to their lves (#26, p. 3)."

This large segment of our population can become our best disciples and certainly a strong force in doing evangelism and carrying out ministry in the community. Seniors have a built-in respect and esteem. They have the wisdom that comes through life experiences, and they are saints in their own right. They can conduct lay counseling and Bible studies and work with new believers. It is much easier for those over 65 to say, "I love you," and to express Christian love than for any other age category.

Trouble doll number six is perhaps the most fascinating. Again, the church growth people teach that 75 to 90 percent of those active in church today first came through a friend, relative or associate already in church. Further, the average church member can identify at least seven unchurched friends and associates. Every one of our congregations, then, has the opportunity of ministering to a group of people seven times the size of the active membership of the congregation. We need to expand our vision of what the parish is and to whom we can minister God's care and love. In doing so, and as we affirm our members in witnessing in their daily lives, we can reach the horde of people who are just waiting to be invited into the congregational family.

The Guatemalan Indians share their troubles with their dolls and during the night the dolls try to solve them. Those called to witness can sleep tonight too, for God will turn every one of those six troubles into an opportunity for witness tomorrow.

Our members have friends and family to invite into the kingdom. While our population is getting older, this can provide a great resource for doing ministry in the community, the Baby Boomers and Busters are searching and we can fill their needs for a more meaningful life. These are walls which need to come down so we can discover the marvelous richness as we kingdom people become one in Christ. Many of our congregations are in a state of decline or passivity, but we can move them with God's spirit to be alive, dynamic, inviting enclaves of God's kingdom again. We must continually send out missionaries all over the world: that is indeed our global mission. But, we have wonderful opportunities right here where we live to bring the unchurched into the kingdom as well.

Let's wake up from our sleep and find that our troubles are really joys and opportunities of the kingdom!

References

Toward Developing an Evangelistic Lifestyle. Valley Forge, Pennsylvania: The American Baptist Churches in the USA. 1972.

Arn, Win. "Have You Checked Your Ratios Lately?" *The Win Arn Growth Report,* #3. Monrovia, California: Church Growth, Inc. 1984.

Arn, Win. "Five Stages of Life-Cycle Churches." *The Win Arn Growth Report. Monrovia, California: Church Growth Inc. No date.*

Arn, Win. "The Church's Challenge and Opportunity of an Aging America." The Win Arn Growth Report, #26. Monrovia, California: Church Growth, Inc. No Date.

Hunter, George G., III, "What Are the Facts About Growing Churches?" *Church Growth America.* March-April 1982.

Hunter, George G., III. "What Kind of Churches Reach Secular People?" *The Win Arn Growth Report,* Win Arn, Ed., #33. Monrovia, California: Church Growth, Inc. 1991.

Lintern, Paul. Guidelines for Newspaper Writing. Unpublished manuscript (handout). Communications Committee, Ohio Synod, LCA. ca. 1979.

Luther, Martin. *The Small Catechism in Contemporary English,* Philadelphia, Pennsylvania: Fortress Press. 1968.

Navarro, Billie, Mrs. "ELCA Schools: Advance Evangelism Goals." *The Evangelizing Congregation.* Chicago, Illinois: The Division for Congregational Life, Evangelical Lutheran Church in America. Fall 1989.

Pallmeyer, Paul, Ed. "Did You Know?" *The Evangelizing Congregation.* Chicago, Illinois: The Division for Congregational Life, Evangelical Lutheran Church in America. Spring 1989.

Schaller, Lyle E. *Activating the Passive Church: Diagnosis and Treatment.* Nashville, Tennessee: Abingdon. 1981.

Schmalenberger, Jerry L. *Lutheran Christians and Their Beliefs: Book II.* Lima, Ohio: Fairway Press. Copyright by St. John's Lutheran Church, Des Moines, Iowa. 1987.

Towns, Elmer. "How To Go To Two Services." From a flyer from Church Growth Institute advertising videotapes by the same title. Lynchburg, Virginia. No date.

Walker, Charles, Ed. Quotations from Kirby Page's *Living Joyously* (Rinehart), #109. *Speakers' Illustrations for Special Days.* Nashville, Tennessee: Abingdon. 1956.